IT WAS ALWAYS A CHOICE

IT WAS ALWAYS
A CHOICE

Picking Up the Baton of Athlete Activism

DAVID STEELE

TEMPLE UNIVERSITY PRESS
Philadelphia / Rome / Tokyo

TEMPLE UNIVERSITY PRESS
Philadelphia, Pennsylvania 19122
tupress.temple.edu

Library of Congress Cataloging-in-Publication Data

Names: Steele, David, 1964– author.
Title: It was always a choice : picking up the baton of athlete activism /
  David Steele.
Description: Philadelphia : Temple University Press, 2022. | Includes
  bibliographical references and index. | Summary: "This book
  contextualizes the latest rise in athlete activism against racial
  inequality by surveying the history of protest in American sports.
  Steele reveals that the platform sports stardom affords has always come
  with the responsibility to speak out against injustice even if not all
  athletes have answered that call"— Provided by publisher.
Identifiers: LCCN 2021059338 (print) | LCCN 2021059339 (ebook) |
  ISBN 9781439921739 (cloth) | ISBN 9781439921753 (pdf)
Subjects: LCSH: African American athletes—Political activity—History. |
  African American political activists—History. | Professional
  athletes—Political activity—United States—History. |
  Sports—Political aspects—United States—History. | Sports—Social
  aspects—United States—History. | Racism—United States—History. |
  BISAC: SPORTS & RECREATION / Cultural & Social Aspects | SOCIAL
  SCIENCE / Ethnic Studies / American / African American & Black Studies
Classification: LCC GV706.35 .S755 2022 (print) | LCC GV706.35 (ebook) |
  DDC 796.092/396073—dc23/eng/20220209
LC record available at https://lccn.loc.gov/2021059338
LC ebook record available at https://lccn.loc.gov/2021059339

Printed in the United States of America

9 8 7 6 5 4 3 2 1

TO EVERY ATHLETE

who ever has, and ever will,

stand, kneel, or speak for what is right

and against what is wrong.

May you forever choose wisely

and courageously.

The way I go about my life is I set examples. If it inspires you? Great, I will continue to do that. If it doesn't? Then maybe I'm not the person you should be following.

—**MICHAEL JORDAN,** 2020,
in *The Last Dance*, acknowledging that he did once spurn
a request to endorse a Democratic candidate by saying,
"Republicans buy sneakers too"

The no. 1 job in America, the appointed person, is someone who doesn't understand the people and really don't give a fuck about the people.

—**LEBRON JAMES,** 2018,
on President Donald Trump, in a pre—All-Star
Weekend documentary

CONTENTS

IT WAS ALWAYS A CHOICE

INTRODUCTION

> The artist must take sides. He must elect to fight for
> freedom or for slavery. I have made my choice. I had no
> alternative.
>
> —PAUL ROBESON, June 24, 1937,
> in a speech at London's Royal Albert Hall denouncing
> fascism during the Spanish Civil War

By 1937, Paul Robeson was well into his theater and film career. The movie version of the stage sensation *Show Boat* had come out a year earlier; 1933 had seen him showcased in *The Emperor Jones*. He was still more than a decade away from the U.S. government's quest to bury his performing career as punishment for what it claimed were traitorous remarks—remarks that it called upon none other than Jackie Robinson to refute in front of a congressional committee.

Robeson's athletic career was even further behind him. He had left Rutgers University in 1919 after earning letters in football, basketball, baseball, and track and becoming a two-time All-American in football. His last year playing the sport—after three seasons in the National Football League, even before it officially took on that name, and long before it instituted its "gentlemen's agreement" against signing Black players—was 1922.

Sports had put him on the national radar, but his many other pursuits throughout segregated America had kept him there.

In 1937, those pursuits put him on the stage at Royal Albert Hall in London, with numerous dignitaries and celebrities supporting the side of democratic rule during the Spanish Civil War. Authors Virginia Woolf and C. S. Lewis were in the audience. Pablo Casals was broadcast in from Bucharest. The program for the event was designed by Pablo Picasso. Robeson, however, was the marquee name, the face and voice the organizers wanted most to pack the biggest punch.

They knew that he could move the crowd like none other, and only in small part because of his unmatched, world-renowned baritone. Nothing defined Robeson's life at that point more than his utter fearlessness. He had been the only Black student at Rutgers when he enrolled, just the third ever to attend, and was the first ever on the football team; the day he reported to practice, his teammates attacked and beat him severely enough to break his nose and dislocate his shoulder. Four years later, his presence defined the program and the university.

For this event, Robeson had planned on recording a speech to be played over the loudspeakers. When organizers expressed fears that the opposition would try to jam the signal (and that Robeson's broadcasting from Russia, where he was speaking and performing, would send the wrong message on such a night), Robeson hit back by recording his speech anyway—and then traveling to London to give it in person.

It was, as expected, a thunderous rebuke of fascism, racial and ethnic oppression, and tyranny against not just the common people but their art, culture, education, and individual expression.

At the heart of Robeson's speech were the words that begin this introduction. He reinforced those ideals with this statement:

Every artist, every scientist, every writer must decide now where he stands. He has no alternative. There is no standing above the conflict on Olympian heights. There are no impartial observers.

By then, to repeat, he was thirty-nine years old. He no longer was running, throwing, hitting, or leaping for his or any other country, for a scholarship or a paycheck, or for the admiration of the crowd or the scores of a judge. Technically, he didn't need to add *athlete* to *artist* or the other professions.

But athletes had sides to take and choices to make too. They did in the 1940s and 1950s, when Robeson was blackballed and saw his livelihood and freedom taken away. They did in the years before and after his death in 1976. They did at the turn of the twenty-first century, and they do to this day.

Those who did, and do, choose Robeson's path have become as immortal as he is. And then . . . there were those who decided that they had an alternative, who thought that they could stand above the conflict.

They generally believed that they had chosen to say nothing.

They were wrong, and Robeson was right. Their choice had told the world everything.

1

THE CHOICE

Use Your Platform—or Don't

We're having a moment in sports right now.

The definition of *right now*, of course, changes by the week, the day, the minute . . . the moment. Right up through the writing of this book in 2021, incidents that shook the world as we had once known it were happening constantly. They moved people to decide, over and over, whether they would fight to change the world that they'd known or use their power to keep it exactly as it was.

In just one week in America, the second week of April 2021, a young Black man in a Minneapolis suburb was shot dead by a police officer—the head of the local police union, in fact—during a traffic stop over an air freshener hanging in the rearview mirror. A Black Army lieutenant was pepper-sprayed, pulled from his car, and beaten by another pair of officers, this time in southern Virginia, during another traffic stop, this time over a temporary license tag on a new car. Video of Chicago officers shooting and killing a thirteen-year-old boy was released . . . and it made the prosecutor and the mayor who supported him out to be liars, after they had claimed that the child had pointed a gun. The volume is overwhelming at a given moment, and it would be impossible for an activist to greet each act anew with the individual outrage that it deserves. But no more do such events fly under the radar or seem like anomalies, thanks to a sea-change event whose anniversary and the markedly changed reaction it brought to every similar tragedy afterward were being marked.

All of these events happened as the trial of the Minneapolis cop who had kneeled on the neck of George Floyd nearly a year earlier was drawing to its conclusion. The guilty verdict, coming in a week where so much brutality remained obvious, proved to be the one crucial clue that something had changed, the payoff of the work of the previous year for some, the previous five years for others, and the previous hundred years for still more.

All news concerning the police, their victims, the public protests, and the reactions to them was viewed through the lens of Floyd's death: how he died, who killed him and how, who watched it unfold in front of them and recorded it for the world, the insistence by the authorities that no one had seen what they actually saw, the too-familiar hunger for those authorities to protect the killers in uniform and the power that they represented . . . and, most of all, the worldwide movement that sprang from the outrage against the public, broad-daylight, on-camera slaying of an American by the state.

It was a movement, it was a revolution, it was a reckoning.

And it wasn't even the beginning. Because while Floyd's murder in the late spring of 2020 was the lens through which the present, near future, and distant future were and have to be viewed, the resulting movement can't be seen clearly without the lens of a much quieter, less explosive, utterly nonviolent moment some four years earlier.

That moment was Colin Kaepernick kneeling. Except that, in the beginning, it wasn't even that: It was Colin Kaepernick sitting.

It was an NFL quarterback, well known and going through a low point in his meteoric career. It was a quiet decision on a crowded sideline in a somewhat-crowded stadium in a preseason game in which few outsiders had much interest—not in the results or the stats, much less the conduct of the injured players in the minutes before kickoff.

Before the game, while "The Star-Spangled Banner" was playing.

Only a handful of people noticed. Only one asked Kaepernick why after the game. When everybody found out, the timeline of events that led to where we are today began.

That timeline included everybody taking sides. And that universe included every athlete in America and many around the planet.

They all had to choose. They had to choose a side, and they had to choose whether to take a side. Choosing to not take a side in the era before Kaepernick would be perceived as a default choice, no choice at all. But this was an illusion of the time, unique in American sports history and manufactured by the neglectful choices of the top athletes of the 1980s, 1990s, and 2000s.

In the decades prior to that, athletes like Paul Robeson had long known about the choice facing athletes, as human beings with the power to command public awareness and attention and leverage their unique economic and cultural position to demand change. Kaepernick reminded the sports world of that reality and inaugurated a new age of American athletes discovering and using their power. It once again became clear that an athlete's decision to not take a stand for social change is a choice in itself, and it's always clear which side that athlete has chosen.

The athletes who did not engage in activism also had to choose to explain their choice . . . and that choice spoke volumes too. Plenty of athletes decided to keep their reasons to themselves. That told the world more about themselves than they might have realized (unless they realized what it did say about them, and their silence was good enough for them).

Many important athletes had been able to play and perform their entire lives, always in the public eye in one way or another, without ever having to take a stand on anything even a fraction as substantial as the conditions in which Black people live and die. Their positions as American sports celebrities had afforded them luxury that they constantly enjoyed, even when they weren't conscious of it.

Kaepernick had that luxury, and he gave it up. In doing so, he became the face of a generation . . . of athletes, of that special exalted level of celebrity, that public figure in an even more rarified air of fame, recognition, and influence. He was impossible to ignore. It was impossible to avoid taking a position on him. It became more impossible to, one way or another, avoid taking a position on what he stood for.

Just as it was impossible to predict that Floyd's public execution would be the last straw for the masses, who decided that they'd had enough, the final length of the long fuse that finally ignited the powder keg, it was impossible to predict that the fuse that led to the 2020 uprising would be lit by the singular, specific figure that was Kaepernick. Certainly, no one drew "Preseason Week 3" in the office pool as the moment when he would decide that enough was enough.

What a nation of athletes chose to do in the wake of Kaepernick's action would mark them from that moment on. Immediately ahead lay a full National Football League (NFL) season. In a remarkable historic twist, so did a presidential election, with a pair of candidates who, in winning or losing, would break with precedent and tradition in ways that were obvious at the time and that would prove even more obvious throughout the next term of the presidency and beyond.

Also laying ahead were a pair of reckonings that, in their time, were as impactful as the one five years later and that laid an important piece of the groundwork in the movement generated by Floyd's killing. The national wrestling with the police murders of Alton Sterling and Philando Castile in July 2016—a little more than a month before Kaepernick's first protest—was already underway. Their resolution and the aftermath, and the dominos that fell along the way, were permanently intertwined with the ongoing Kaepernick saga.

Those extrajudicial slayings had been Kaepernick's last straw. He was not alone in his horrified, furious reaction—not alone among onlookers to the pair of recorded crimes, and not alone among athletes, or even NFL players. In fact, less than a week after the killings, a quartet of athletes with unquestionable international catchet had ascended one of the largest platforms available to them to call the world to task about those issues. On July 13, less than a week after the two killings, National Basketball Association (NBA) superstars LeBron James, Chris Paul, Carmelo Anthony, and Dwyane Wade stood onstage in Los Angeles at ESPN's annual nationally televised ESPYS awards show and sounded, in James's words, "a call to action to all professional athletes." Paul invoked the names of groundbreaking athletes of the past and declared, "We choose to follow in their footsteps."

At the time, the stance by the four future Hall of Famers seemed like the peak of athlete engagement. Even with the open-ended challenge to their peers, nobody particularly foresaw who would accept the challenge, or how. In hindsight, though, the direct link from the four NBA All-Stars' modest stand at the ESPYS in reaction to Sterling's and Castile's killings and the culmination of that tumultuous spring week in 2021 cannot be understated.

Castile's hideous, intimately filmed death at the hands of police in another Minneapolis suburb and the subsequent acquittal of the police officer who shot Castile dead in the driver's seat of his car led directly to Kaepernick's social media posts condemning them, to his protest, to the years of athlete activism that ensued. Those protests created a different set of social conditions following Floyd's killing in the city itself, a new groundwork of activism that led in turn to the trial of his killer. The death of another young Black man in a different suburb during, like Castile, a traffic stop, in the middle of the aforementioned trial, opened a new chapter.

None of those happenings took place in a vacuum. They were not isolated. They followed back and forth on a continuum—one that had existed for more than a century before but certifiably moved on the same line through Kaepernick and his decision to do something about it.

The date on which Kaepernick was first witnessed sitting down during the national anthem isn't marked off and immortalized. It's not stamped in lore, American or otherwise, the way the Fourth of July is, or September 11, or (for a painfully recent example) January 6. Even the date of Floyd's death can be recalled with relative accuracy—it was May 25, but more notably, it was Memorial Day, and the video of his killing began to spread by the end of that day and had raced around the planet by the end of the next day.

The conditions surrounding Kaepernick's moment, however, were as unexceptional as could be. Again . . . Week 3 of the NFL preseason, with only the biggest diehards paying close attention to the schedule and focusing on the games and who was and wasn't playing. It was Friday evening, August 26, 2016, at Levi's Stadium in Santa Clara, California—the host stadium for Super Bowl 50 less than six months earlier—with the home team San Francisco 49ers playing the Green Bay Packers.

In the Associated Press game story that night, the 49ers' former starting quarterback was a topic of some interest . . . but only enough interest to be mentioned for the first time in the fourth paragraph. Kaepernick was still recovering from surgery on his left shoulder that had ended his previous season—he had missed the second half of the 2015 season with a torn labrum in his left shoulder. The 2012 season, in which he had taken over the starting quarterback job late and led the 49ers to their first Super Bowl in nearly two decades, wasn't that long before, but a lot had transpired in his career and the team's life since. He was playing for a new coach (Chip Kelly) and, potentially, his job, depending on how soon he would return to health and his previous form.

From the 2016 Associated Press story on ESPN.com:

Colin Kaepernick did not fare as well as he looked extremely rusty in his first game action since last November. He completed 2 of 6 passes and generated one first down on three drives.

"I wish we had done a little bit more but it was good to get out there and get my feet wet," Kaepernick said.

Even though Kaepernick struggled after sitting out the past two weeks with a tired shoulder and Blaine Gabbert led the Niners to a touchdown on one of his two drives, Kelly said he's not ready to pick a starter for the season opener against the Rams on Sept. 12.

"You're never going to make any decisions walking off the field," Kelly said. "We'll sit down as a staff and see where we are."

It's hard to imagine who even read that story that night, or the next day. It's the official record of Preseason Week 3 Niners–Packers, to be sure, but it's unlikely that many people went out of their way looking for the account, not even people curious about how Kaepernick looked in his first game action since the previous October.

The story that the NFL's own website ran, though? It will be studied forever—not only for breaking the news of Kaepernick's protest but for being a shining example of eyewitness reporting and explanatory journalism. Credit goes to the NFL Network's reporter, veteran newspaper beat writer and broadcaster Steve Wyche, one of (still) a handful of Black journalists regularly covering the NFL, locally or nationally.

Additional credit goes to Jennifer Lee Chan, a camera operator for what was then the NBC Sports Bay Area network, who took a wide shot of the field during the anthem and, afterward, noticed that Kaepernick was the only player in uniform not standing and was, in fact, sitting on the bench with his head bowed, completely inconspicuous. Chan tweeted the photo that backed up the story that Wyche told about Kaepernick.

With Kaepernick soon taking the counsel of former NFL player and Green Beret Nate Boyer that kneeling rather than sitting would convey his message and eliminate the prospect of showing disrespect to the military, Chan captured the first and only image of Kaepernick sitting as the anthem played. Kaepernick will be forever associated with the image of kneeling, but thanks to another nonwhite journalist noticing one anomaly among more than a hundred players in an otherwise forgettable game, that singular image has its own place in the history of the movement.

After the game, Wyche spoke to Kaepernick alone, away from other reporters, and asked what he had done and why. Kaepernick answered with blunt simplicity and clarity.

In his article "Colin Kaepernick Explains Why He Sat during National Anthem" on the NFL website, Wyche writes:

> "I am not going to stand up to show pride in a flag for a country that oppresses black people and people of color," Kaepernick told NFL Media in an exclusive interview after the game. "To me, this is bigger than football and it would be selfish on my part to look the other way. There are bodies in the street and people getting paid leave and getting away with murder."
>
> Kaepernick said that he is aware of what he is doing and that he knows it will not sit well with a lot of people, including the 49ers. He said that he did not inform the club or anyone affiliated with the team of his intentions to protest the national anthem.
>
> "This is not something that I am going to run by anybody," he said. "I am not looking for approval. I have to stand up for people that are oppressed. . . . If they take football away, my endorsements from me, I know that I stood up for what is right."

Kaepernick said that he has thought about going public with his feelings for a while but that "I felt that I needed to understand the situation better."

He said that he has discussed his feelings with his family and, after months of witnessing some of the civil unrest in the U.S., decided to be more active and involved in rights for black people. Kaepernick, who is biracial, was adopted and raised by white parents and siblings.

What Kaepernick did in the game, how he played after his long, injury-induced layoff, surfaced in the next-to-last paragraph of Wyche's story, the same sort of afterthought that the Associated Press had innocently and unwittingly given him.

In hindsight, Kaepernick's choice is a turning point in American history. It became even more of one than the previous most prominent sports protest that had used "The Star-Spangled Banner" as its canvas: the raised fists by Tommie Smith and John Carlos on the medals stand at the 1968 Olympic Games in Mexico City. That was no small feat. Smith and Carlos's silent demonstration during the medals ceremony that night was the culmination of more than a year of planning, under the auspices of the Olympic Project for Human Rights (OPHR), organized by them and their mentor and college professor Dr. Harry Edwards, with the intent of driving home a specific, detailed message about the plight of Black America and ways to address it. The world had known for months that the Olympics were about to become a stage for that message. Kaepernick, by comparison, thrust himself to the forefront of his cause in less than two months.

That, in turn, was the precursor to an even more potent turning point: the Floyd protests four years later. But at the time, it was Kaepernick's personal stand, one that it's now obvious that he didn't originally intend to be public, or at least as public as it became.

Yet it doesn't take hindsight to see the chain reaction that it caused because it began immediately, and nobody could avoid it, even if they tried—and, clearly, the very act of trying to avoid it was a choice, a statement, in itself. One man's choice called a league, a sport, an athletic universe, and a universe in total to declare their choices as well, and to do it quickly.

Kaepernick's decision will define him forever. As he said, he thought it out, and it clearly was informed not just by his whole life to that point but by the horrible events of that summer. But it was still a decision in a moment that freezes him and his stance in time.

He was ready for it. That was clear then and would become even more clear as the days, months, and years went by.

The others who made choices in response showed how prepared they were, and how not prepared.

Every teammate, fellow NFL player, and, eventually, athlete at every level had to choose whether to join him in open protest or to refuse and then justify their refusal. Such refusal meant alignment with the oppressors, oppressors all the way up to the soon-to-be president of the United States. It meant satisfaction with the status quo. Kaepernick had a place in sports and in society, and he needed to learn to stay in it, the idea went. The anthem was to maintain the precise status that it had enjoyed in the context of the game for decades. The introduction of the military into the pageant— whether introduced voluntarily by the powers-that-be in sports or paid for by the U.S. Defense Department only within the past few years specifically for marketing the joys of enlistment—was to be protected at all costs.

And, most relevant to Kaepernick's stated reason for protest, the role of police, and their immunity from accountability, their license to kill was to be preserved. Country, flag, troops, law enforcement, every other pillar of the American hierarchy that was beneficial to the white power structure and was lethal to the entire Black populace regardless of salary or celebrity . . . the continuation of that role was what the athletic world and its individuals were standing for with their silence, detachment, and acquiescence.

The athletes, starting with Kaepernick's fellow 49ers teammates and NFL brethren, were the first to declare themselves.

Safety Eric Reid decided quickly that he agreed with Kaepernick, what he did and said, and why. He wasted little time in joining him, forming a visible alliance with his quarterback: In the 49ers' next (and final) 2016 exhibition game the following weekend, Kaepernick kneeled for the first time, taking Boyer's advice, and Reid kneeled next to him. They kneeled together for every game of the 2016 regular season, sometimes just the two of them, other times with another supportive teammate.

One of Kaepernick's former teammates, center Alex Boone, chose differently. As a member of the Minnesota Vikings by then, Boone gave several interviews in the weeks following Kaepernick's first protest. He claimed that he was choosing his words carefully. He also used the template for outrage established long before this protest—one used every time an individual unapologetically bucks the system by co-opting the most visible symbols of that system. He made sure, for instance, to point out that he had a brother who had served in the military. He also declared that because his brother and the rest of the soldiers throughout history had fought for the freedom of all American citizens, then Kaepernick had no right to exercise that freedom to critique American society.

Boone's reaction (here from *USA Today*) was not unexpected or particularly original:

> That flag obviously gives him the right to do whatever he wants. I understand it. At the same time, you should have some (expletive) respect for people who served, especially people that lost their life to protect our freedom. . . . We're out here playing a game, making millions of dollars. People are losing their life, and you don't have the common courtesy to do that. That just drove me nuts.

Joel Dreessen, then of the Denver Broncos, took his emotions a step further, noting that if Kaepernick had been on his team and on his sideline expressing himself this way, he would have "stomp[ed] on his toes" to get him to stand for the anthem.

The very nature of his protest, of course, lent itself to categorizing the reactions along racial lines. Boone and Dreessen are white.

Jim Brown is definitely not. For decades at that point, Brown had been a paragon of Black athletic resistance, from the very same era that produced Smith and Carlos. He personified individual expression and refusal to obey the laws of society for the sake of obedience by the very brevity of his Hall of Fame football career—he called a halt to it after the 1965 season, just nine years in, and moved into another profession on his own terms. His was one of the names mentioned regularly as coming from a period that would never be duplicated and against which future generations of better-paid Black athletes would always be unfavorably compared: Muhammad Ali, Bill Russell, Kareem Abdul-Jabbar, Tommie Smith and John Carlos, Jim Brown.

Days after Kaepernick first sat, Brown declared that "I am with him 100 percent." However, he wavered in that first expression of support, agreeing with Kaepernick's cause but not his method of fighting for it. At a panel discussion on the NFL Network, Brown said (according to ESPN.com):

Now if you ask me "Would I do that?" No I won't, because I see it a little differently. I'm an American citizen. I pay my taxes. I want my equal rights. But this is my country, and consequently I don't want to open up for ISIS or anybody that will take away what we've already gained.

In the ensuing year, Brown spoke less as someone behind Kaepernick's cause "100 percent" and more like someone who believed that his true loyalty was to the flag that supposedly Kaepernick was not respecting enough. In the summer of 2017—after a number of events connected to football revolving around the still relatively new President Donald Trump—Brown told the website *The PostGame*, "I don't desecrate my flag and my national anthem. I'm not gonna do anything against the flag and national anthem. . . .

Colin has to make up his mind whether he's truly an activist or he's a football player."

Brown made these remarks around the time that players across the NFL were grappling with Trump's latest condemnation of Kaepernick and everybody in and around the league who supported his cause. In September 2017, in a speech campaigning for a senatorial candidate in Alabama, Trump infamously declared, "Wouldn't you love to see one of these NFL owners, when somebody disrespects our flag, to say, 'Get that son of a bitch off the field right now. Out. He's fired. He's fired!'"

Kaepernick, by then, was not on an NFL roster, the unofficial, unwritten blackballing of him by teams having begun when he opted out of his contract and became a free agent in early 2017. Players around the league still kneeled in support of him and his cause, or stood with fists raised, or sat as he had in his original protest. Trump condemned all of them. Players, en masse, retaliated the very next week—and the likes of Brown faced another bevy of cameras and microphones asking what it all did or should mean. Kaepernick's activism once again was revealing the choice that had gone under the radar since Brown's prior era of political relevance—but was there all along.

Brown was bringing additional baggage to this specific conversation by now. Before his inauguration, Trump had anointed Brown as one of the Black luminaries to whom he would bestow an invitation to Trump Tower in Manhattan to discuss whatever he believed that the segment of Black America who supported him needed to hear. This group included another Hall of Fame football player, Ray Lewis, and entertainers Kanye West and Steve Harvey. After the visit, Brown said of Trump, "I fell in love with him."

Not long after, as the inauguration approached—and as the venerated John Lewis, civil rights frontline fighter and congressional representative from Georgia, castigated Trump and announced that he was boycotting the ceremony—Brown leaped to Trump's defense and spoke demeaningly and condescendingly of Lewis.

"When I hear him cry the blues about Mr. Trump and saying it's an illegitimate presidency, I take offense to that," Brown said in a live interview on CNN. "Don't cry the blues because you did not get the vote out and this man had a genius way of winning the election."

For many reasons—including his abhorrent record of abusing women and showing little or no remorse for it—Brown's status as a sports-activism icon was not a closed case. As one objection to Kaepernick followed another in the years after the first protest, Brown made it clear that he had chosen where he wanted to stand in the most powerful movement of this era. Everything he had done previously stood to be revisited with a much more critical eye. That included his gathering of Black superstar athletes and activists in 1967 in Cleveland—during his postcareer establishment of his business and Hollywood life—to query and support Ali in his fight with the government over his refusal to enter the military draft.

The room full of Black public personalities at the height of their political power made for an iconic photo. Ali had died earlier in 2016, months before Kaepernick's protest began. The surviving participants in the meeting, the faces left in the photo, all had their chance to weigh in on Ali's legacy, on Kaepernick maneuvering in the same territory decades later, and on the carryover of their own beliefs through the long stretches of life and the acquisition of years of wisdom.

Brown announced where he now stood. Russell was also in the photo, seated at the front table with Ali and Brown. Russell, the Celtics center who transcended basketball to define winning with eleven championships won as a player and to be the first Black coach of a team in a major American pro sport, answered by posting a photo of himself on his various social media accounts, kneeling in support of Kaepernick.

Abdul-Jabbar, also seated at the table on the other side of Ali from Russell, had in a sense already shown where he stood through his numerous public commentaries earlier that summer about the same police atrocities that had pushed Kaepernick to action. The first editorial that he wrote, about Kaepernick sitting during the anthem in the exhibition game, was published days later in the *Washington Post*. Abdul-Jabbar writes that Kaepernick "behaved in a highly patriotic manner that should make all Americans proud."

"What should horrify Americans," Abdul-Jabbar states, "is not Kaepernick's choice to remain seated during the national anthem, but that nearly 50 years after Ali was banned from boxing for his stance and Tommie Smith and John Carlos's raised fists caused public ostracization and numerous death threats, we still need to call attention to the same racial inequities. Failure to fix this problem is what's really un-American here."

What happened in those fifty years and how that compared to what happened before and after is the subject of this book.

Thanks to changes in media, in the spread and access of information, it was even easier to immortalize a decision, to freeze a choice in time, in 2016—as the discussion grew surrounding Kaepernick and police brutality and American injustice and fundamental racial oppression—than it was in 1967, when Brown and Abdul-Jabbar and Russell and Ali shared a conference table and a discussion about war and patriotism and obligation. It became easier to record those choices for posterity in 2017 and so on, through the horror of a police execution recorded on a cell phone in 2020, and through the trial of that officer and an escalated surge of white domestic terrorism in 2021.

The new opportunities to show and learn about the daily persistence of inequalities and violence that Black Americans have long faced in turn provided opportunity after opportunity to pick a side. The former backup quarterback of the 49ers picked a side and almost didn't get noticed for it, but then suddenly was. As the years sped along, the Jim Browns and Kareem Abdul-Jabbars and Bill Russells and Dak Prescotts and LeBron Jameses and Stephen Currys and Candace Parkers and Maya Moores and Charles Barkleys and Jerry Rices and Drew Breeses and Brett Favres and Tom Bradys and Cam Newtons and Tiger Woodses and Naomi Osakas . . .

. . . and the NBA and the NFL and the Women's National Basketball Association (WNBA) and Major League Baseball (MLB) and the U.S. women's national soccer team and, somehow, with almost no warning, NASCAR . . .

. . . all picked sides. Some did it by picking both sides. Others did it by picking no side. But a side is what they took.

The choice only partially related to the flag, the anthem, and the men and women in the military. At its core, what side they, and everybody, chose spoke to what and who athletes are.

Are they living, breathing, angry, frustrated, flesh-and-blood humans who have a platform that comes with their visibility and relative wealth, and the hunger of their team owners and fans to see them perform, and the capacity to change the world from what it is to what it should be? Do they know and understand that platform? Do they recognize their leverage as would-be cogs in a system built on their backs and designed to contain and control them?

Or are they there to put on a show for you, to be taken out of their boxes long enough to entertain and then be put away until needed again? Were they put on this planet, on this continent, and in this society to shut up and dribble?

That was the choice Kaepernick asked athletes to make, by silently sitting and kneeling, back in 2016. It's the choice that everyone has now.

It's the choice that has defined every era of sports, and every athlete who has played them, since sports in this country have existed.

2

COLIN KAEPERNICK AND
HIS SPIRITUAL PREDECESSORS

As he said to the NFL Network's Steve Wyche at the beginning, Colin Kaepernick knew that the consequences of his decision to protest could be severe. Athletes, celebrities, and everyone with something tangible to lose understand that; it's the reason that they regularly give for staying away from challenging statements or actions, if they give one at all. Kaepernick, though, also understood this from the education that he had undertaken to reach his decision. The cultural footprints left by Tommie Smith and John Carlos are easy to see, even for someone who isn't a student of the history of activism. They, in turn, followed the footprints left by others, and their own footprints had been followed by others before Kaepernick, who had learned firsthand about the toll it would take.

Smith and Carlos willingly became brothers in the fight for racial justice and equality and the elevation of human rights worldwide . . . even though they were not particularly close otherwise. The most contentious moments of their relationship have made their differences seem more severe than they really are. What those differences illustrate more than anything, though, is that two men from differing backgrounds, traveling separate paths to a shared destination while experiencing similar events and influences, can produce a result that will stand for eternity. They arrived at the fight from opposite directions, but they went through the same travails to get there and cared about reaching their goal above everything else.

As much as their arrival on the medals stand in the infield of Mexico City's Estadio Olímpico Universitario on October 16, 1968, is occasionally portrayed as a quirky coincidence—one of the things that Smith and Carlos differ on is how they ended up sharing one pair of black gloves, for instance—there was never any doubt about why they were there and whether they would have still chosen to be there if given a chance. (Both men have never wavered in saying that they would do it all over again.)

Over and over, to reinforce the meaning of their joint gesture on behalf of Black America and victims of oppression around the world that night in Mexico City, Smith and Carlos have come together—for awards and honors and commemorations and anniversaries—to stand together as they did in their athletic youth. If they weren't physically in the same place, their beliefs were always joined. Their unique personalities are reflected in their speech and mannerisms—Carlos an extroverted product of the streets of Harlem, Smith an introverted product of the fruit and vegetable fields of central California. Both have never shied away from taking on the mantle of responsibility for the ensuing generation of athletes who wanted to follow their lead and show that they understood where they were walking.

Thus, when the world began to process Kaepernick's sit-down, his kneel-down, and his words, it turned to both Smith and Carlos. It quickly learned that both men had connected, separately, with Kaepernick. Kaepernick had a decent grasp of what the two men had done, why, and how—and, as he had said to Wyche, he had done his homework and was open to doing even more. The connection was in plain sight. The 49ers had a consultant on staff for the players, coaches, and staff who was the ultimate expert on athletes and activism: Dr. Harry Edwards, author, San José State University professor, renowned public speaker, and originator of the Olympic Project for Human Rights (OPHR). The protest on the victory stand during "The Star-Spangled Banner" in 1968 was the end result of conversations hosted and plans laid out by the OPHR, spearheaded by Edwards and the student sprinters at San José State as those Olympics approached.

As Kaepernick had said, he had not run his idea past anybody beforehand, but he had engaged in numerous sit-down meetings with Edwards to better understand his own feelings and his desire to act over the bloody summer of 2016. After he began protesting, Kaepernick had not only a mentor for his efforts to focus his words and actions but also a primary source for direct and indirect action, and for studying the historical background of such action.

Edwards, of course, became as much of a go-to voice for Kaepernick as Smith and Carlos were, and in return, he brought a level of firsthand knowledge to an athlete who had access to him, and vice versa. Again, as with Smith and Carlos in Mexico City, Kaepernick and Edwards's proximity was serendipitous. Edwards made sure that what he said, to the public and to Kaepernick, counted.

"If you go back to 1968, and the whole year that I spent framing up The Olympic Project for Human Rights, I did that so that when a protest was made, people would understand the message," Edwards told the ESPN website *The Undefeated* a few weeks into the 2016 regular season.

"One of the things I've been trying to do, and not just with regards to Kaepernick but this whole [civil rights] effort, whether it's the Seattle Seahawks, or whether it's LeBron [James] and CP3 [Chris Paul] and [Dwyane] Wade and Carmelo Anthony, is to frame up the concerns so that their efforts make sense."

James, Paul, Wade, and Anthony had made their own joint declaration about the police brutality of that summer. The Seahawks, like every National Football League (NFL) team finding what its players individually and collectively believed was their responsibility suddenly in the spotlight, wrestled with what they wanted to express and how best to do it.

In 1968, the messaging by Edwards, Smith, Carlos, Olympics teammate Lee Evans, and others on the topic of the upcoming Olympics was always on point and in concert. Kaepernick benefitted from that lesson.

Smith and Carlos also stayed as on-message with all their media calls about Kaepernick as they had fifty years earlier. More critically, they sought out Kaepernick themselves, out of far more than curiosity. Both men had committed the majority of their post-sprinting lives to teaching, in classrooms and in every other possible venue. The rough patches in their lives have been well documented, many of them direct consequences of others' reactions to their outspokenness, their activism, and that singular act on the medals stand. Despite that, though, if there was a student of their activities who needed to understand the paths that they had taken before and after, they both were eager to teach.

From separate directions, Smith and Carlos talked to Kaepernick; supported his organization, the Know Your Rights Camp, established to educate youth on the legal framework that affected their lives and freedom; and detailed the similarities between their stands and the choices they made.

When Carlos met Kaepernick in person a year later and posed with him, he told the *TMZ Sports* website that Kaepernick "ha[d] cemented his status in my books as one of many great individuals whose name will be spoken alongside the likes of Muhammad Ali, Jackie Robinson, Dr. Tommie Smith, Peter Norman, and myself."

Around that same time in 2017, Smith and Kaepernick met for the first time, as part of the production of a documentary on Smith's life, *With Drawn Arms*, which premiered in 2020. The two also posed for a photo.

By the time the two icons met with the quarterback, Kaepernick's days of kneeling before NFL games were over. He was well into the first year of his exile from the sport, still unsigned by a team halfway through the season, overlooked and unapproached in favor of starters and backups far less accomplished than he (in a handful of cases, players with no experience in the NFL, and in one case, Jay Cutler of the Miami Dolphins, signed out of retirement).

Both Smith and Carlos knew of exile, having been expelled from the Olympic Games after their protest in 1968, never to compete internationally again. Coincidentally, the last time that both appeared as active athletes in their prime was . . . as pro football players—Smith with the American Football League's (AFL's) Cincinnati Bengals and Carlos with the NFL's Philadelphia Eagles. Kaepernick, as of this publication, has never played a game of NFL football since the finale of the 2016 season—January 1, 2017, two months after his twenty-ninth birthday.

The threat of exile, subtle or overt, always hangs over the athlete willing to engage in open, public activism, and the authorities in sports have followed through often enough to give the threat real teeth. Smith and Carlos's expulsion from Mexico City was on the less-subtle side; Kaepernick's ongoing, career-ending rejection by the thirty-two NFL teams always came with a level of plausible deniability. (Those plausible denials are not to be confused with the completely implausible ones, such as the one floated by nationally renowned NFL reporter Peter King in 2017 after conversations with unnamed 49ers staffers: "There are those in the building who think Kaepernick might actually rather do social justice work full-time than play quarterback." The notion that Kaepernick had spurned the NFL instead of vice versa persisted for years among people who wanted him to never play again.)

The banishment of Muhammad Ali in 1967 did not appear at the time to come with an expiration date. On the day when he refused entrance into the U.S. Army, he was stripped of his boxing license and his world heavyweight title, and it wasn't clear that either would be reinstated, even if he capitulated to the government's wishes. He did not capitulate, and not until the New York State

Supreme Court ordered that his boxing license be reinstated could he return to his livelihood. It was another year—in June 1971, three months after the "Fight of the Century" against Joe Frazier at Madison Square Garden—before the U.S. Supreme Court overturned his draft-evasion conviction. Technically, his time barred from his sport did not rob him of his career, but it robbed him and the world of what would have been the heights of his career.

Similarly, when Kaepernick no longer received offers to play, he was in the prime of a career that had already seen him play in the Super Bowl. Tom Brady won the Super Bowl that concluded the 2020 season at the age of forty-three; a month later, the Saints' Drew Brees retired after having just turned forty-two. At the time of that Super Bowl, Kaepernick was thirty-three, presumably far from the end of his career, even without the presence of outliers like Brady and Brees. He was four years removed from his last snap in the league.

The aforementioned Paul Robeson was long separated from his athletic peak as a pro football player by the time he had his passport revoked by the U.S. government in 1950. Robeson had played pro football in the early 1920s, before a gentleman's agreement would shut all Black players out of the ranks of the pro leagues for decades. Early in 1949, the legendary orator had been quoted by a wire service as declaring in a speech in Paris that Black Americans would never fight for the United States against the Soviet Union ("quoted by" being the operative phrase, in hindsight, as the record of the remark remains dubious). It was the beginning of the U.S. government's campaign—via the State Department and the House Un-American Activities Committee, among other entities—to officially denounce his embrace of Communism and his ceaseless demands for the human rights of Black Americans. Robeson appealed to have his passport returned several times in the ensuing years as his performance bookings overseas dried up. As with Ali, it took a Supreme Court decision for Robeson's passport to be returned to him so he could resume travel and performing. It finally came in 1958, when he was sixty.

Blackballing has always been a convenient tool for the powers-that-be when their control of their primary moneymakers is openly challenged. Its effectiveness in the sports community—which presents itself as a true meritocracy in which results are the only measuring stick used and where statistical measurements have grown only more prominent throughout the decades—is extraordinary considering how available objective numbers supposedly dictate decisions. In the cases of Ali, Smith and Carlos, and Robeson, those powers could point to an infraction of a known rule or policy violation to explain why they'd been banned, whether one agreed with it or not.

With Kaepernick, though, no policy was broken. The NFL had no rule concerning how players should behave during the pregame anthem. Yet the goalpost was moved when and where it was needed to keep the doors locked and Kaepernick on the outside. National Basketball Association (NBA) players Craig Hodges and Mahmoud Abdul-Rauf could relate.

Hodges's erasure from a significant portion of the NBA's historical narrative accelerates every year, despite the publication of his 2017 autobiography, *Long Shot: The Triumphs and Struggles of an NBA Freedom Fighter.* In terms of team and individual accomplishments, Hodges can hold his own with Kaepernick's resume. He played in the NBA for ten seasons; led the league in three-point shooting percentage three times (in an era when teams were often blessed if they had even one three-point threat on their rosters); won the All-Star Weekend three-point contest three straight years, from 1990 to 1992; and played a pivotal role in winning the first two championships by the Michael Jordan–led Chicago Bulls, in 1991 and 1992.

At thirty-two, after that second championship, the Bulls released him. No team picked him up. He played in Italy, Turkey, and Sweden afterward, and he spent a year in the U.S. minor leagues, but he never played another NBA game. The only team to hire Hodges as an assistant coach (in 2005, thirteen years after his playing career ended) was the Lakers team coached by Phil Jackson, his coach in Chicago and one of the few NBA figures to publicly object to his apparent blackballing. He rarely is mentioned during the annual three-point contest despite still being tied for the most lifetime victories. He is virtually absent from the ten-hour documentary on the Bulls dynasty that aired on ESPN in 2020.

That NBA career ended after his trip to the White House after the 1992 championship, in the traditional visit with the president, at the time George H. W. Bush. Hodges made a point to write a letter to hand to Bush, asking him to make a definitive change because "300 years of free slave labor has left the African-American community destroyed."

Predicting how long quarterbacks' careers can last, just by the devastatingly violent nature of the sport and the position, is almost impossible. The same holds true for a boxing career, even for a champion like Ali. But in basketball, shooters can shoot almost forever; age thirty-two is no more of an indicator that the end is imminent for a shooter than age twenty-nine is for a quarterback. The Bulls, in fact, were masters in deploying specialists like John Paxson and Steve Kerr throughout their dynasty. Of course, that supply of alternatives alone can make a player like Hodges expendable—and going against the grain of what's acceptable for athletes in celebratory, intentionally benign circumstances like White House championship celebrations is exactly the type of thing that makes players like Hodges expendable.

Like his forebears and the generation who followed, Hodges made his choice with full knowledge of the potential consequences. Blackballing is always a possibility.

Abdul-Rauf knew the possible consequences as well. His six seasons as a Denver Nugget—and the two years in college during which his offensive prowess became well known—were defined by his high level of play. He was a starter and averaged more than twenty points per game for the Nuggets. Even the relative ease with which the basketball public adjusted to his name change after his conversion to Islam early in his career seemed like a sign of a societal evolution, considering the consternation that had ensued when first Ali and later Kareem Abdul-Jabbar changed their names and espoused their religious beliefs.

However, when Abdul-Rauf's decision to abstain from standing at attention for the pregame national anthem late in the 1995–96 season became known—much in the fashion that Kaepernick's became known, through an observer noticing his absence and wondering why—his future immediately was thrown into jeopardy. The calls came for the NBA to not just suspend him but ban him for life. In the end, the Nuggets traded him in the off-season. He bounced around the NBA and teams in Europe for several years after that and walked away from the sport occasionally. But once he had made his decision related to his faith, the anthem, and society at large, NBA teams were reluctant to commit to him. As in the case of Kaepernick, the record shows that they never blackballed him, but reality tells a different story.

Kaepernick began his protest alone but was joined by players scattered across the NFL (and, eventually, athletes and other activists and demonstrators across the planet). He was also joined each week of that final 49ers season by teammate Eric Reid . . . who also suffered the consequences when teams went to great lengths to avoid signing him, twice. He stayed with the 49ers for the first year after Kaepernick left, 2017. He became a free agent after that season, and no team showed serious interest in him until the 2018 regular season had begun, when the Carolina Panthers signed him. In his last 49ers season and his two seasons in Carolina, he kneeled before every game. The Panthers released him after his second season. In a league perpetually in search of safeties, with the position taking on more requirements and responsibilities and demanding arguably the widest variety of skill sets of any single position, Reid got no interest in the off-season.

Then, during the 2020 season, his former Panthers coach, Ron Rivera—now the head coach in Washington and with the kind of power over all football decisions that most (if not all) coaches envy—offered to sign Reid to the team's practice squad. Reid had been a starter during those two years in Carolina and had played well enough to easily earn a contract extension after his first season there. Washington needed safeties badly, either as a starter (Landon Collins had suffered a season-ending injury) or for depth. The league had made rosters more flexible that season as it forged through the COVID-19 pandemic; theoretically, spots on the practice squad would mean a potential path to the main roster in this season more so than in any other season.

Reid clearly was a starting-quality safety, never mind worthy of signing a real NFL contract and moving immediately onto the depth chart of a team that was in serious need of talent at the position and ended up muddling through the season just below the break-even mark. A better record and a better team, with a player who had proven his worth on the field and with his convictions, seemed like a worthwhile goal.

Washington never said why they did not offer Reid a full roster spot in a season of need. Nor did any other team in the NFL. And NFL teams have not earned the benefit of the doubt regarding their motivations. Said Reid himself to the Associated Press, "I just don't think playing on the practice squad is reflective or indicative of my career." His point was valid. Nobody's explanation as to why he was not given that roster spot was nearly as persuasive as Reid's performance on the field. Neither were the predictable reactions from many—that Reid should have been grateful to even get a call to join a practice squad after not having a job at all. It was clear that his unemployment had little to do with his ability or production. Once again, a sport that presents itself as a meritocracy, as one that adheres at least in some part to objective criteria, made a decision that reeked of subjectivity, one that distanced it from an activist who kneeled to show his advocacy for equal human rights. Reid was back to being blackballed. At the time of this writing, in the final month of the 2021 NFL regular season, Reid still was out of work.

He was twenty-eight when he played his last NFL game, one year younger than his former 49ers teammate and kneeling partner was when his career ended involuntarily.

Reid still will go onto the permanent record as having provided the ultimate support to an aggrieved teammate. That's no small feat in itself. Instances of entire teams standing behind one player or one cause have happened enough times in history to be acknowledged and revered. Individual stances, in both individual and team sports, also have earned their place in immortality.

The athletes who, like Reid, buck the majority in defense of a teammate are rarer.

Even more rare, at that time and in that climate, was the position that a backup catcher for the Oakland Athletics staked out at roughly the same time, in September 2017: an athlete taking a knee in a sport where, in that particular year, it was estimated that only sixty-two players in Major League Baseball (MLB) were Black. Bruce Maxwell, one of that scant number of Black players, kneeled in front of his dugout as the anthem played before a game, with his white teammate Mark Canha standing at his side, with a hand on his shoulder.

It was seen as a potentially watershed moment, the first, and long-awaited, leap of the movement from the sports most populated by and popular with Black America to the one that annually had to explain why it was losing connection with that same segment of America and had lower representation with each passing year.

The potential of that moment basically disappeared almost immediately, not to even raise its head slightly for three more years. Maxwell spent the next four years on the fringes of the majors, on and off the A's major league roster, then released, then unsigned, then in the Mets organization briefly. The number of Black players on major league rosters did not grow appreciably in the meantime, and it was not until the summer and fall of 2020, when the whole sports world followed basketball in reacting to the Jacob Blake shooting in Kenosha, Wisconsin, that other baseball players began making their feelings known by kneeling or even sitting out games.

The backdrop of flags and anthems stood out once again in Maxwell's protest. One unnamed baseball general manager told *Sports Illustrated* in 2018 that Maxwell's inability to find a job was best attributable to his decision to kneel during the national anthem—even more so than an arrest on assault charges in the previous off-season.

The easy conclusion to make from the risk level of standing up is that the larger the platform is, the safer it is to use. Plenty of examples back that up. LeBron James's career has survived and flourished, as his ways of pushing the issues have expanded in recent years, right through the year when George Floyd's killer broke precedent by facing consequences for his actions. So has that of Megan Rapinoe, among the very best soccer players on the planet and the most vocal and active. Kaepernick's career did not survive; Reid's did only sporadically. Hodges and Maxwell disappeared.

Yet Ali had the most coveted individual title in sports on Earth taken from him in the prime of his life. Smith and Carlos literally stood on a podium elevated above their competition in the Olympic Games, when it was even more once-in-a-lifetime than it is today—and they were told to leave the Games and not return, going unembraced by this country's Olympic movement until decades later, and still vilified by many when their protest is remembered.

The stakes are enormous. It's still rare that the stage of the person taking them on is big enough and sturdy enough to handle them. But enough athletes have been willing to take a stand, no matter what, to give Kaepernick a blueprint. Enough athletes have been in a position to take a stand for the universe around the Kaepernicks of the world to make an informed choice.

Even the ones who seemingly drew the blueprint, though, had a blueprint to follow. The pioneers who changed the world just by showing up and staying put cleared a path for the rest to follow.

3

YOUR PRESENCE IS AN
ACT OF PROTEST

Jack Johnson, Joe Louis, Jesse Owens,
and Jackie Robinson

The roots of the white nationalism, rigid racial hierarchy, and brutal suppression and oppression of nonwhite people that define the United States as we know it today reach at least back to the arrival of Europeans on the continent in the fifteenth century and their extermination of the native population and their importation of Africans to be enslaved in the seventeenth century. Within that timeline, the history of athletes fighting to reclaim those rights on behalf of their race is a blink of an eye. The period in which nonwhite faces have even existed within the universe of the major sports organizations hasn't been much longer.

It hasn't been much more than a century, in fact. Jack Johnson won the world heavyweight boxing championship in 1908. Jesse Owens won four Olympic gold medals at the Berlin Games in 1936. Joe Louis became the heavyweight champion just a year later. Ten years after that, in 1947, Jackie Robinson made his Major League Baseball (MLB) debut. Pro football had only begun readmitting Black players in 1946. Pro basketball had only been sporadically integrated in the two decades before the fully merged

National Basketball Association (NBA) began signing Black players in 1950.

The big public and private colleges in the South did not see serious integration in football and basketball until the mid- to late 1960s; many of their counterparts in the North were quicker at integrating, but example after example prove that even these Northern counterparts were far from progressive in the treatment of their Black players. Paul Robeson played football for a major East Coast institution in the late 1910s and in the still-forming National Football League (NFL) in the early 1920s, and tales of horrific mistreatment are integral to both experiences.

Taking a principled stand as an athlete on issues beyond their own participation in their sport was a concept decades away from full development. In the grand scheme of sports and what they represented in, and about, American society, the mere existence of Black faces in overwhelmingly white spaces was an act of rebellion in itself. What shook the country to its foundations was the notion that Black people, and nonwhite people overall, could simply *be*. Until those pioneers gave the nation a chance to see Black athletes excelling alongside their white counterparts, sports for Black people meant being in your own place, living among, teaming with, and competing against your own people. The Negro Leagues. The all-Black pro football circuit. The Harlem Globetrotters. In one form or another, separate organizations for tennis, golf, and track and field. Separate colleges, universities, and trade schools for Negroes.

And, for decades, even while Johnson fought, and after his career was over and his freedom had been snatched from him, Black heavyweights would still mostly have the opportunity to fight just each other, only on the rarest occasions fighting white people, and never for the world title.

For everything that Johnson represented to American society overall, to white society and to Black society, the most disruptive thing that he did—what shone the light on every other disruptive act of his life—was simply to be an adult Black man functioning in a world that did not want him to function in it and was not equipped or prepared to reckon with his success and endurance.

The title of the excellent 2004 Ken Burns–directed documentary *Unforgivable Blackness*, and the accompanying biography by Geoffrey C. Ward, is drawn from an editorial by none other than W. E. B. Du Bois, in the August 1914 edition of the National Association for the Advancement of Colored People (NAACP) periodical the *Crisis*:

> Boxing has fallen into disfavor—into very great disfavor. To see publications like the *New York Times* roll their eyes in shivery horror at the news from Paris (to which it is compelled to give a front page) makes one realize the depths to which we have fallen.
>
> The cause is clear: Jack Johnson . . . has out-sparred an Irishman. He did it with little brutality, the utmost fairness and great good nature. He did not "knock" his opponent senseless. Apparently, he did not even try. Neither he nor his race invented prize fighting or particularly like it. Why then this thrill of national disgust? Because Johnson is black. Of course, some pretend to object to Mr. Johnson's character. But we have yet to hear, in the case of white America, that marital troubles have disqualified prize fighters or ball players or even statesmen. It comes down, then, after all to this unforgivable blackness. Wherefore we conclude that at present prize fighting is very, very immoral, and that we must rely on football and war for pastime until Mr. Johnson retires or permits himself to be "knocked out."

Besides providing a title for an entertaining and informative biography on the champion nine decades later, the great Du Bois brilliantly skewers the panic that Johnson perpetually inspired among white Americans. By 1914, Johnson was already in exile, escaping the consequences of his conviction on federal charges of violating the infamous Mann Act, which was used to punish interracial relationships. He was boxing overseas to avoid arrest and imprisonment and to pay his bills and retain the championship that he still precariously held. On the occasion that Du Bois so wryly describes, Johnson had won a twenty-round decision over Frank Moran (a Pittsburgh fighter of Irish descent) in Paris. It was a fight that Johnson only took, according to the *Unforgivable Blackness* book, because the norms of the day dictated that only a white competitor would draw the crowd and produce the revenue to make the bout worthwhile—the public would not accept a bout against the top title contender, Sam Langford, because both he and Johnson were Black.

The *New York Times* had scoffed at the very idea of the Paris fight for weeks, ridiculing it as a money grab for the desperate Johnson, and the morning after Johnson's win, it did, in fact, devote space on the front page of its June 28, 1914, edition for two stories on it. The main story calls the bout a "farce" and "positively the poorest bout ever staged as a championship event." It emphasizes that the less-than-sellout crowd hooted at Johnson and called the fight a "fake." It also refers to Johnson as "Black Fighter" and "Negro" in the subheads, presuming that by that time, its audience was unaware of Johnson's race.

Du Bois, clearly, could not resist poking fun at the shrill condemnation of Johnson, using the pretext of critiquing the bout itself and wondering how the previously much-admired sport of prizefighting had suddenly become such an immoral cesspool—especially compared not only to other sports but to the other events developing in the nation and the world. (In fact, the events that led to the start of World War I were already taking place when Du Bois wrote his piece.)

Considering how long Johnson had been on the national and international radar by then, that "Blackness" had left an indelible impression on the minds and psyches of white America, or at least on those who chronicled it for daily consumption.

The public travails and trials of Johnson serve as landmarks in the history of sports and society. He had to leave the country to earn the heavyweight title for the first time, over Tommy Burns in Sydney in December 1908. The 1910 knockout of "Great White Hope" Jim Jeffries in Reno set off one of the worst outbreaks of white violence in the nation's history, as white Americans retaliated against Black people in cities from coast to coast for their perceived loss of racial pride.

The beatdown of Jeffries, in turn, inspired Congress to pass laws prohibiting the transportation of films of prizefights across state lines. Until Johnson's prowess and reputation grew, and certainly before he defeated Jeffries, films of great fights were a huge draw and a great aid to the spread of both boxing and motion pictures as popular and lucrative forms of entertainment. Afterward, the sport was denounced as indecent and unworthy of exposure to good citizens whose morals could be corrupted. In fact, the move to put an end to showing and shipping fight films began with the championship bout in Sydney—the sight of a Black man, never mind the despised Johnson, rendering a white world champion senseless and inert on the canvas, was considered so objectionable by those recording the fight that the film abruptly ends just as Johnson throws the final punch. By all accounts, Burns being counted out and Johnson's arm being raised in victory have never been witnessed on film.

The difference was the presence of Johnson and his dark skin.

As reprehensible as the government's misuse of the aforementioned Mann Act was, it still did not personify the true objection that white society had to Johnson. It wasn't far off, of course— the Mann Act's purpose was to halt organized prostitution and solicitation-related crimes, so it outlawed taking women across state lines "for the purpose of prostitution, debauchery, or for any other immoral purpose." The charges were fitted to Johnson for dating and marrying white women in public without reservation, shame, or attempt to conceal it. It achieved the desired effect, particularly when Johnson fled the country after his conviction and later lost his heavyweight crown after roaming the world, seeking title bouts and money and avoiding arrest.

His crime, of course, was living his life as he pleased. That choice also served as his method of protest, even if nobody at the time, and very few since, have claimed it as such. One of the very few to so claim it is Kenneth Shropshire, the chief executive officer of the Global Sports Institute at Arizona State University and a lifelong scholar of the intersection of sports and society.

Said Shropshire to the *Sporting News* in 2018: "Even if you don't think he was making a societal protest, and you look back at the thought of the day, from even the *Crisis* [magazine] and the NAACP and everybody saying, 'He's not good for us.' . . . But was he, in fact, making a bigger statement than anybody else was making at the time—'I'm free. I'm free to do what I want to do'?"

That was part of the irony of Du Bois using the pages of the *Crisis* to scold the American newspapers for their pearl-clutching over Johnson. The guardians of respectability in Black America in the early part of the twentieth century largely condemned Johnson and his overt brashness. This reaction foresaw similar admonishments in later years from the same segment of the population, toward both the community's overexuberance over landmark events in Black sports history and the activist athletes themselves. In Johnson's case, Booker T. Washington was routinely appalled by the champ's activity—he once said that Johnson was "doing a grave injustice to his race. . . . A man with muscle, minus brains, is a useless creature."

Such condemnation from either white or Black society never appeared to faze Johnson, and that aspect of his personality is what made him unique for his time, and for any time.

James Earl Jones, who played a Johnson-like character on Broadway and in Hollywood in *The Great White Hope*, notes in the Burns documentary: "He wouldn't let anybody define him. He was a self-defined man. And this issue of his being Black was not that relevant to him. But the issue of his being free was very relevant."

Johnson was still globetrotting to avoid jail when he fought Jess Willard in Havana in 1915 and was beaten, losing his heavyweight title. The next time a Black man was allowed to fight for the same crown was twenty-two years later, in 1937, when Joe Louis beat James J. Braddock in Chicago. That long drought after Johnson's demise was not an accident. It was no accident that Louis himself, the top contender for years even after a loss in his initial bout with Germany's Max Schmeling, had to wait as long as he did to get a title shot—even though, when he got it and won, it made him the youngest heavyweight champion ever at the time, at age twenty-three.

Again, the magnitude of a Black man holding that title—in the 1930s, and in the aftermath of Johnson's reign—could not then and cannot now be overstated. Black auteurs throughout the decades have captured the glee that ran through Black America as Louis won, and then repeatedly defended, his crown, from Langston Hughes to Count Basie to Richard Wright to, more than a decade after Louis's death, Spike Lee (in a scene from his feature *Malcolm X*).

In winning the championship and then knocking out Schmeling in their rematch, a revered symbolic victory over Adolf Hitler and Nazism, which had held Schmeling up as a symbol of Aryan supremacy, Louis never had to say or do anything for or about the cause of equality in America. The consequences of doing so were likely, even in hindsight, to have been viewed as disastrous for him and Black people at every level of society. It's impossible to imagine that his words would have even been represented fairly, accurately, and with any allowance of dignity to Louis himself. As is detailed in Chris Mead's 1985 biography, *Champion: Joe Louis, Black Hero in White America*, his words would have been rendered unreadable because writers of the day habitually recorded his comments in what the author calls "Uncle Remus dialect." It was less a poor interpretation of Louis's thick Alabama accent and more the routine of the white press of the day treating all Black speech this way, along with portraying him as slow, lazy, and sullen, a brute just a few steps removed from animals who came by his ferocious punching ability naturally as opposed to through hard work, technique, and perseverance.

Louis was famously instructed by his handlers, especially his publicity agents, to keep his public speaking to a minimum and to be scrupulously careful about his public appearances. Whether they were set down as specific rules or not, Louis's camp generally did agree that he was not to have his photo taken with a white woman and that he was not to appear in a nightclub alone. He was not to even give a hint that he was gloating over an opponent in victory. His habit of not smoking or drinking alcohol was emphasized. He was to keep a blank expression in interviews and when photos were taken. All of it, in particular the first admonition regarding white women, amounted to an anti-Johnson campaign. They all took on added importance once he won the title and after he won the Schmeling rematch, when he was accepted by broader 1930s and 1940s society as the conqueror of the Nazis and upholder of the best American values and ideals.

None of this meant that the nation's admiration of Louis translated to the elimination of racism and improvement in treatment and opportunities for the rest of Black America. It did not mean that Louis himself or his family would benefit, other than from the living he made from fighting. It did yield a less toxic image of Louis's race when it was seen as personified by him and his accomplishments and behavior. That was no small feat because the hatred of Johnson was projected onto Black people across the board—which is why the Black intelligentsia of the day were so concerned about how he acted and whether that would reflect on them.

This is where Owens's effect on America landed as well. Louis's rise up the boxing ranks coincided with Owens's emergence as the crown jewel of the new class of Black Olympic stars. Like Louis's, Owens's victories over competition from Nazi Germany, on German soil and in full view of Hitler in the stadium, worked flawlessly as pro-American propaganda and as a source of pride among

Black people, who were closer to being recognized as true, legitimate Americans than they ever had been. They had fought the first two significant battles for the United States against the Nazis—even while government officials were working to keep their distance from the approaching war in Europe and while some of them were openly allying with Germany. The two Black titans of sports had won. It offered at least a whiff of hope for equality.

But, like Louis, Owens was rewarded with very little—almost none, really—of that equality when he returned to America and American society. Black America embraced him as it did Louis and exalted him as the best of them. White America was content with what the two athletes represented of America but had zero interest in them as people and as members of a broader, just population. Yet Owens had succeeded despite the obstacles that his own country had put in front of him, and that meant an honored place among his people. Thus, like Louis, he never had to say a word or commit an act to advocate for an end to oppression to secure their pride.

When Louis joined the U.S. Army barely a month after Pearl Harbor, his role in the war effort was clearly defined—he was not on his way to battle, but his role in boosting morale, with exhibition fights as fundraisers and on military bases for the troops, was invaluable. The army did not prioritize his placement among the soldiers to whom he would be most inspirational, his Black brothers in arms. They did not have them in mind when they considered how Louis could be useful to his country. That doesn't mean, though, that he didn't have a direct hand in helping Black Americans in a time of need. An underlying critical character in the tale of Jackie Robinson's military career was, yes, Louis.

In his 1971 autobiography, *I Never Had It Made*, Robinson tells of applying for Officers Candidate School soon after he was drafted in the early days of the war. He was assigned to Fort Riley in Kansas, and his unit in the segregated army had to wait out an inexplicable delay in being admitted to the school. Three months passed, and Robinson chalked it up to "my first lesson about the fate of a

Black man in a Jim Crow Army." But after Louis was transferred to Fort Riley, Robinson and members of his unit appealed to him—and suddenly the logjam cleared, and they joined the training, with Robinson eventually becoming a second lieutenant.

History occasionally mixes up two similar incidents involving Robinson. Louis was never involved in the segregated bus incident on a base in Texas that ended with Robinson's getting court-martialed (and later acquitted, before he received an honorable discharge). Louis was involved in a similar situation regarding segregated seating at a base in Alabama that he was visiting, in which he got the army to uphold its own rules that overrode the local laws.

Across the country and around the world, in between his morale-boosting boxing exhibitions, Louis witnessed constant unequal treatment for Black soldiers and used his influence to fix it. The U.S. Armed Forces were not integrated until after World War II, but it is unlikely that they would have even taken a step in that direction had the most famous Black athletic celebrity in the country not volunteered to join the army early on. For the most part, their integration flew under the radar, but it would set a precedent in the coming era.

Louis returned to the boxing ring after the war's end in 1945. Later that year, Robinson was signed away from the Negro Leagues to play for the Dodgers organization. In 1946, the year when Robinson played in the minor leagues in Montreal, Johnson died in a car accident. The world had changed in the four decades since Johnson had emerged as a notably fearsome specter in the minds of white society. It had also been changed by the war, as some factions in America were finally seeing the flaws in the philosophy that the country was a bastion of freedom for all but simultaneously justified in treating Black people as second-class citizens, regardless of how they had labored to help win the war and how conclusively their prowess at the nation's most celebrated contests had been proven.

Much had not changed, however. When Robinson agreed to be the player to reintegrate organized baseball, he struck a similar bargain to the one Louis had accepted a dozen or so years earlier. He would have to begin his baseball life, in the minors and eventually the majors, by turning the other cheek to the atrocities that would be visited upon him. There were going to be guidelines to his behavior—not the same as the ones Louis lived by, but from the same mindset. Success for a Black man in a white world that would grant the least acknowledgment possible of his presence would depend on his not doing anything to offend that white world or lashing out at what it said and did to him. So, Robinson would have to remain silent—as the legendary conversation between him and Dodgers owner Branch Rickey went (according to Robinson's autobiography):

"Are you looking for a Negro who is afraid to fight back?"

"I'm looking for a ballplayer with guts enough not to fight back."

The statement that Robinson was required to make—and willingly chose to make—was one that would allow him to make few, if any, verbal statements at all, certainly not about the state of racism and oppression in the game or in society. His presence was the statement, and in time his excellence would be one as well.

Like Louis, Robinson had already made a statement just by being close to a paragon of virtue. Robinson did so before ever knowing that he had been evaluated for exactly those virtues. The nationwide search that Rickey had quietly conducted for the player to integrate the game prioritized strength of character, preferably through multiple trials. Robinson had plenty of those, dating back to his childhood and proceeding through his career as the rare nationally known Black football superstar while a student at UCLA, as a former Negro Leaguer, as an army officer, and as the central figure in a court-martial over the segregated seating. He had a world of experiences and a record of navigating land mines (figuratively) and coming out intact, alive, and with his dignity and determination unbowed. He was accustomed to fighting and winning.

The twist, though, was suppressing the outward physical act of fighting for as long as it took. Rickey expected it would be a year in the minors and two in the majors, and despite numerous potential detours, that's how long the guidelines lasted. The connection between the lifting of the restrictions that Rickey had placed on Robinson's behavior, mandating that he turn the other cheek, and Robinson's subsequently winning the only Most Valuable Player (MVP) award of his baseball career had never been explicitly made. Robinson hints at it in his autobiography when he speaks of the pressure finally being lifted—but there is no doubt that after he no longer had to turn the other cheek, he reached his baseball, and likely his athletic, peak. It is also little if no coincidence that once he did begin speaking out again, he did not stop for the rest of his life.

Robeson, it is worth repeating, had advanced from his original platform of athletics long before dominating the stages of the theater, movies, and social and political advocacy. He was commanding his latter platforms in 1949 when he was dragged into the debate over whether his demands for equality for his people—regardless of the method or circumstances—should be labeled as treason. That year, Robinson was dragged into that same debate. After having survived the segregationist nature of the South, the West Coast, college life, the military, and professional baseball, he was now called upon in the middle of his pivotal third Dodgers season to denounce Robeson's reported remarks about Black Americans fighting for their country against Communist Russia. Specifically, he was asked by the head of the House Un-American Activities Committee to "give the lie" to Robeson's comments.

It served as a fascinating plot twist in the tale of Black advancement through society and, tangentially, sports. It required yet another profession of patriotism, love, and respect for the country in its time of need, even while that same country had never done anything but mistreat and disrespect them and their people. That thread runs back to Johnson as much as to all the others: The momentous 1910 bout with Jeffries, which triggered the terrorism of Black communities in the aftermath, took place on the Fourth of July.

The thread runs very obviously through Owens's and Louis's standing in for the nation against the Nazis. It runs through Louis's and Robinson's wearing the uniform of the U.S. Armed Forces, enhancements of their acceptance as heroes. It runs through the ensuing decades to the 1968 Olympics, to sitting and kneeling and walking out and turning a back to the flag and the national anthem.

In this instance, it ran through two proud, strong accomplished Black men who were pitted against each other, with the government hoping to use one to destroy the other. Robinson did not want to do it, but he did testify before Congress, emphasizing that he did not believe that any one man could speak for fifteen million Black citizens and that he would not be tempted to throw away everything that he believed that he was entitled to in this country "because of a siren song sung in bass."

Robinson's testimony was something that he would later say he did not regret, but he admits in his autobiography that he had "grown wiser and closer to the painful truth about America's destructiveness" and that he respected Robeson even more for his sacrifice because "I believe he was sincerely trying to help his people."

The blackballing of Robeson began in earnest the following year, in 1950. The attempt to use one Black hero as a weapon against another was largely a success, despite Robinson's efforts to mitigate his criticisms—ultimately, the committee got the headline that it wanted. The pattern of measuring the value of Black people by their professions of loyalty to America was set further in stone. Some two decades later, Owens was asked to prove his loyalty to his country—again, after he had proven it in multitudes already without reciprocation—by going to talk to Tommie Smith, John Carlos, other Black U.S. Olympic athletes, and their supporters after the medals-stand protest.

The contributions by all of them to the cause by their mere presence in places where they were not welcome cannot be overlooked, and the movements and advances that followed could not have been taken without them. Because of these athletes and their sacrifice, the steps to the next stage of evolution were shorter. But as future generations of Black athletes took the next critical steps beyond mere existence on the same field as their white counterparts, the legacies of these pioneers for whom that constituted such a significant step in itself would be invoked as if that mere existence ought to be enough, repeating the tactic of pitting athlete against athlete.

4

STAR-SPANGLED RESISTANCE

From Rose Robinson to the Bubble

Colin Kaepernick's act of resistance and the movement that it launched gave the world a new opportunity to reacquaint itself with Jackie Robinson's autobiography—specifically, a remark in the preface that in the four-plus decades since its publication had never garnered that much attention.

It comes at the end of the preface, Robinson's reflection on what he has seen, felt, and thought since the opening game of his first World Series, capping the end of the groundbreaking 1947 season:

> There I was, the Black grandson of a slave, the son of a Black sharecropper, part of a historic occasion, a symbolic hero to my people. The air was sparkling. The sunlight was warm. The band struck up the national anthem. The flag billowed in the wind. It should have been a glorious moment for me as the stirring words of the national anthem poured from the stands. Perhaps it was, but then again perhaps the anthem could be called the theme song for a drama called "The Noble Experiment." Today as I look back on that opening game of

my first World Series, I must tell you that it was Mr. Rickey's drama and that I was only a principal actor. As I write this twenty years later, I cannot stand and sing the anthem. I cannot salute the flag; I know that I am a Black man in a white world. In 1972, in 1947, at my birth in 1919, I know that I never had it made.

Kaepernick himself posted parts of the Robinson quote from time to time during his year of protest on the National Football League (NFL) sidelines and in the years afterward. Clearly, these words had gained more poignancy since their publication and in the context of what Kaepernick was enduring. Everybody who understood what Kaepernick was doing—why the flag and the anthem were the symbols of choice to use as his canvases, and why his opposition immediately leaned into castigating him as an enemy of the state for not showing the appropriate level of patriotism—could relate to what Robinson said.

On the other hand, those who had long ago reduced Robinson to a static, bloodless object lesson, a plaster saint sacrificed to the gods of racial tolerance and understanding, had missed his recognition of the duality of flag and song: its representation and objectification for Black America. There were numerous declarations that Kaepernick and the athletes supporting him were an insult to Robinson's memory; his stoic, silent stance from the postwar era; and his service to his country while wearing the army uniform. These people were suitably stunned when apprised of his actual words, after a quarter century of reflection and multiple hard lessons about the nation's willingness to recognize the inherent rights and citizenship of his people. No, they discovered the hard way that Robinson would not have stood at attention with hand over heart as Old Glory waved and as "The Star-Spangled Banner" played. He says so, point-blank.

The conflicting emotions described by Kaepernick and his Black supporters, then, went back even further than 1968, when Tommie

Smith and John Carlos used the Olympics' traditional playing of the national anthem for its medals ceremony as their backdrop for their gesture of protest. A case can be made, in fact, that it went back to the original Black superstar athlete, Jack Johnson. His conviction in federal court in 1913 for violating the Mann Act led him to sail to Europe to avoid prison and to continue fighting and defending his heavyweight crown; he also earned badly needed extra income in stage shows, speeches, wrestling matches, and other appearances. According to Thomas Hietala's 2002 boxing history, *The Fight of the Century: Jack Johnson, Joe Louis, and the Struggle for Racial Equality*, a dispatch from London in August 1913 describes a scene where Johnson "refused to perform under an American flag" and "directed that it be removed and replaced with the French flag." The accuracy of the anonymous report is in dispute; Johnson was routinely the subject of wild reports about his behavior and comments, in the U.S. and elsewhere in his travels. (One example: It was erroneously reported that he had volunteered to fight in the French Army when World War I broke out.) However, in the 1914 bout in Paris against Frank Moran, the one that inspired W. E. B. Du Bois's snarky "unforgivable Blackness" remark, Johnson reportedly "wore the colors of France," presumably referring to his trunks. The crowd at whose size the *New York Times* scoffed, according to this report, included loud Johnson supporters from the French colonies Senegal, Dahomey (now the independent nation of Benin), and the French West Indies, as well as Parisians and other French residents.

Even if for only brief periods, more than a few significant figures in the history of Black athletes had complicated relationships with the major national symbols. Kaepernick's actions brought many of those athletes' moves—and in some cases, the athletes themselves—out of obscurity. The story of Rose Robinson was revived and refreshed as a result, and full credit for that revival belongs to Dr. Amira Rose Davis, an assistant professor of history, African American studies, and women's, gender, and sexuality studies, and co-host of the popular podcast *Burn It All Down*.

Eroseanna "Rose" Robinson was a member of the 1959 U.S. Pan American Games team, a high jumper emerging as a favorite to make the team for the 1960 Olympics in Rome. During the opening ceremonies at a packed Soldier Field in Chicago, Robinson refused to stand when the national anthem was played. It might not have come as a surprise to American track officials—a year earlier, after she had won the Amateur Athletic Union (AAU) national championship and earned a spot on a team traveling to a meet in Russia on behalf of the State Department, she had announced that she had no intention of going.

"I don't want to be used as a political pawn," Robinson said, according to Davis's account on the website *ZORA* in 2019. And use as a political pawn was exactly what the State Department had planned for the predominantly Black meet roster, hoping to counteract the Soviets' then well-practiced and essentially accurate message that the U.S. had no moral leg to stand on as the leader of the free world while so mistreating its Black population.

The U.S. government's retaliation for this Black female athlete's refusal to toe the patriotic line was not unexpected. After her sit-down at the Pan Am Games, she was arrested on tax-evasion charges over a reported $386 debt. She refused to pay on principle, saying that she did not want her taxes to contribute to the nation's commitment to violence at home and abroad. She responded to the subsequent prison sentence by going on a hunger strike, which drew attention to her case (thanks to a memorable photo of her being carried into court because she was too weak to walk) and inspired public pressure to free her.

Between Robinson's battles with the State Department and her commitment to activism off the field, her window to potential Olympic fame closed. Those 1960 Games were where Cassius Clay, Wilma Rudolph, Rafer Johnson, and Oscar Robertson, among others, entered the international consciousness. Robinson likely would have been a track and field teammate of Rudolph, who won three gold medals in Rome and dominated the Olympic Games like few other female sprinters ever have.

Slipping through the cracks of history seems improbable, if not impossible, for any prominent athlete of any color or gender who takes public stands in the presence of the American flag at any sporting events. It goes against the nature of the nation's relationship with its patriotic rituals, the constant pressure for everybody to adhere to them, and the grip that sports have on the public and the meaning embedded in them. Yet Rose Robinson had been largely forgotten until Kaepernick's kneeling and Davis's shining a spotlight on her career.

Toni Smith had largely been reduced to a footnote as well by the time Kaepernick took a knee, less than fifteen years after she had been in the eye of a storm practically unprecedented for a senior basketball player on a Division III team in the suburbs north of New York City. Smith's story was resuscitated as well, and the nation was reminded of her level of commitment to her cause—and the nation's equal level of commitment to silencing her.

Smith (now Smith-Thompson), born and raised in Manhattan, is now a senior organizer for the New York Civil Liberties Union and an education advocate, fighting for the rights of students in the city school system. She also has embraced the spotlight that followed Kaepernick's protests in 2016, booking such speaking engagements as the all-day town hall at San José State's Institute for the Study of Sport, Society and Social Change on the fiftieth anniversary of the Mexico City Olympics protest. On the same panel as Thompson that day was Mahmoud Abdul-Rauf, emphasizing the continuum of activism and persecution rooted in the symbolism of the flag from Smith and Carlos, through Abdul-Rauf and Smith-Thompson, and, finally, to Kaepernick.

Smith-Thompson's reflection on her experience could have been taken verbatim from every other athlete who has ever appropriated the flag and anthem as a platform for their views.

"It was interesting to hear people say, 'You shouldn't protest with the national anthem or the flag, because that's what gives you that right to do it,'" Smith-Thompson said to the crowd in San José. "And then the counter side was, 'Because it gives you that right, then you should do it.' So I really started to think about this notion of having rights being only in this glass case, where you can't touch it."

As a senior sociology major and basketball player at Manhattanville College in the 2002–03 academic year, Smith had spent her entire scholastic and athletic life absorbing the messages sent by the mandatory pledge of allegiance to the flag, the way it was forced into every sporting event at every level, no matter where and who was involved. She saw the flag and anthem customs enforced in schools that had been neglected and underresourced, where students' rights had been trampled, where poverty reigned and families' demands for attention to their needs went unheeded. The buildup of American military jingoism in the year-plus after the September 11, 2001, attacks brought her to a reckoning about those customs as well. When her last college basketball season began, as the players on both teams stood in line at attention as the national anthem played before every game, Smith began turning to face away from the flag.

Her act of defiance went unnoticed until March 2003, when first the local suburban newspaper and then the *New York Times* wrote about it. The reprisals began almost immediately. The first backlash came from fans at road games, who brought flags in enormous numbers to wave constantly before and during the anthem as they shouted and cursed at her. (The most notable such display was, not surprisingly, at a game at the U.S. Merchant Marine Academy.) The most aggressive reaction came from a man, later identified as a Vietnam War veteran, who ran onto the court at another game and stood in front of her, screaming in her face as the anthem played. The photos and videos from that incident went national, raising the volume on her protests even further.

Smith-Thompson has never regretted her choices or actions. She also has never forgotten who was in her corner—and who was not. No Manhattanville teammate ever joined her in her protest, despite the respect that all admitted that she had earned as a senior and a leader on and off the court and on campus. Those teammates, her coaches, and athletic and academic administrators all supported and defended her publicly; years later, she praised the school president for standing by her during the worst of the backlash. But the isolation during the protest itself was impossible for her to ignore. Even though the risk she took was lower than others in her position, because she was not a scholarship athlete, she still feared repercussions throughout the rest of her final season and as she approached graduation. She was never disciplined and did finish the season, but she never stopped feeling the pressure.

And she noticed that only one other player in all of college basketball, female or male, copied her protest that year: Deidra Chatman of the University of Virginia. Hers lasted one game, and none of her teammates joined her, either.

It was the perfect illustration of why the platform of sports wields so much power . . . and why that power can terrify athletes away from using that platform. It also was another lesson on how protective Americans are about both their patriotic symbols and what they are convinced is sports' place in their lives. If the phrase "shut up and dribble" was not in wide use in 2003, the concept was.

"I'm very clear, then, that had I not been an athlete, there would never have been a scenario like this, where I would have been presented with that choice," Smith-Thompson said in a 2018 interview with the *Sporting News*:

> And I think we're having a different conversation now about sports and athletes not being separate from society. I think a large segment of society still wants it to be kind of this escape from reality. But then, it very much still was; there wasn't even a conversation about sports not being an escape from reality. For me, sports is exactly where all of reality played out.

The resurrection of her pivotal position in the timeline of resistance was more than a happy coincidence. Dr. Harry Edwards, of the original Olympic Project for Human Rights (OPHR), wrote to the young under-siege protester in the midst of her turmoil, and she said:

> I wrote back, and he wrote back, and we had a couple of exchanges, where he sent letters but also articles and information. So there was this really valuable source of information for me to get clear on how my protest was connected to the protests before me, to put myself into context with this historical lineage. Dr. Harry Edwards saw my protest as a very important part of passing the baton.

She admits that she was not well versed on the 1968 protest when she staged hers, but she understood it much better after her interactions with Edwards. He was later the person who added her to the fiftieth anniversary town hall at San José State in 2018. Smith and Carlos, of course, were panelists that day as well.

The reactions to Smith and Carlos, at the time of their protest and afterward, did not fit into neat categories. Support for the protest was not unanimous among the Black press at the time, and clearly plenty of white people in America and across sports stood behind them, in the moment in Mexico City and elsewhere. One of those supporters was David Meggyesy, a veteran white linebacker for the then–St. Louis Cardinals of the NFL.

His story is another that has largely fallen through the cracks, but it was important enough at the time to cause a brief stir in a league that was noted for its conservatism and its allegiance to military and patriotic symbolism nearly as much then as it is today (although then without the direct financial implications of today).

After his seven-year career ended, Meggyesy wrote a memoir of his playing days in 1970, *Out of Their League*, which exposed, among other things, the unvarnished racism and resulting locker-room dissension in the league during the tumultuous prior decade. Near the book's end—describing his final season of 1969, a year after the Mexico City Olympic protest—he describes the time when he defied a team policy on standing at attention, facing the flag and holding one's helmet during the national anthem. According to the book, the policy grew out of a newspaper column castigating the players for their sloppy posture during the anthem and blaming it for the previous week's loss.

The next week, all the Cardinals players obeyed the team directive . . . except one.

"I'd thought a lot about this and decided that saluting the flag was ridiculous," Meggyesy writes:

> Every time I even looked at it, I saw only a symbol of repression, so I decided to protest. My original idea was to pull a [Tommie] Smith by raising my right first in the air and bowing my head. Instead, I decided not to salute the flag but to pretend I was nervous for the game. I was aware that if my protest was too obvious I would be severely fined. When the National Anthem started I stepped out of line and began kicking the dirt and holding my helmet down in front of me with my two hands. My head was bowed and I was spitting on the ground and moving from side to side scuffing the ground with my shoes.

Meggyesy had already established himself as an outspoken opponent of the Vietnam War and had been called on the carpet by team owner Stormy Bidwill for his activism in the locker room. After that first game defying the anthem policy, he said he refused to salute the flag for the rest of that season. Newspaper writers, radio hosts, fans, team officials, and teammates trashed him the entire time; one fan, he recalled, came to the railing behind the bench and screamed, "Meggyesy, you goddamn Commie, why don't you go to Hanoi?" Sticking in his mind above all—Meggyesy remembered it vividly nearly fifty years later—was a banner unfurled in the stands in St. Louis during the final home game, mocking him with the team's popular nickname at the time: "Big Red Thinks Pink."

As an early organizer in the NFL Players Association (he was a college teammate of the union's first president, John Mackey) and as someone who has demanded expanded rights, a stronger voice, and proper medical care for players, Meggyesy has nurtured a reputation as a renegade and a resistor.

When Kaepernick began kneeling, Meggyesy called it "wonderful." Seeing teammates, other NFL players, and then athletes in other sports join him in one fashion or another encouraged him even more. Having firsthand experience in being left alone while standing up for a cause, he found the support for Kaepernick within the sport encouraging.

"This puts it front and center into the consciousness of Joe Public," Meggyesy told the *Sporting News*. "It's in the mindset of fans that now, it's not just about that one player. You can't just focus in on that player, you've got to focus on the issues at hand."

Only a fraction of NFL players visibly took Kaepernick's side, yet even marginal support has been proven time and time again to be better than being left alone in protest. The same week that Meggyesy spoke with so much optimism about Kaepernick's NFL brethren joining him, Megan Rapinoe took a knee during the national anthem for the first time. It was on the sideline of her National Women's Soccer League (NWSL) team, the Seattle Reign, before a game against Chicago, the same weekend as Kaepernick's final exhibition game in San Diego.

In that instant, the burgeoning Kaepernick discussion—which, even then, had yet to excavate such past examples as Rose Robinson or Toni Smith—shifted from talk of ungrateful, privileged, wealthy Black athletes disrespecting their country and biting the hand that fed them to . . . something much different. Rapinoe was not in the gray area of NFL stardom and journeyman status—she was a full-blown superstar, the brightest star on a team full of them, a national team that was beloved by its fan base and celebrated by its country every time it won on the world stage, which was often (as recently as the summer of 2015, the year before Kaepernick's protest began, when the U.S. and Rapinoe won the World Cup). Soccer took Kaepernick's protest to the international stage. It crossed over to female athletes and their status and visibility in the sports and societal universe, escaping the pigeonhole in which Kaepernick's critics wished to characterize his actions. Rapinoe was also gay, which chronically rubbed against the grain of what the public believed that sports and competition represented, male and female.

And she was white.

"It's important to have white people stand in support of people of color on this," Rapinoe told the outlet *American Soccer Now* after her gesture. "We don't need to be the leading voice, of course, but standing in support of them is something that's really powerful."

Her decision to kneel then and there, she said, "was very intentional."

The response from the United States Soccer Federation (USSF), the sport's governing body in America, was just as intentional. It condemned Rapinoe, one of its biggest names, that very night.

"As part of the privilege to represent your country," the statement reads, in part, "we have an expectation that our players and coaches will stand and honor our flag while the National Anthem is played."

The statement also includes a pristine example of the "glass case" vision of rights and freedom that Smith-Thompson points out: "In front of national and often global audiences, the playing of our national anthem is an opportunity for our Men's and Women's National Team players and coaches to reflect upon the liberties and freedom we all appreciate in this country."

The USSF, in plain language, was asking its players to show their gratitude for their freedom by obeying its rules against exercising their freedom of expression.

Rapinoe responded by kneeling again at the Reign's next game. Throughout the next five years, in national and international play and at professional games in the U.S., she kneeled, sometimes alone, other times with supporters, sometimes with all her teammates. The national team collectively decided to stop kneeling early in 2021—some nine months after the social reckoning in the wake of George Floyd's killing began. It was also about nine months after the governing body revoked its rule outlawing kneeling, instituted officially several months after Rapinoe had first kneeled. "Black Lives Matter," the USSF declared.

Along the way, Rapinoe's Black teammates were torn. Crystal Dunn, Rapinoe's national team teammate and pro league opponent, was tempted to join her in protest but balked—with some level of despair, even as she told Rapinoe how happy she was to see her doing it—because she thought "it would look differently if a Black girl on the team kneels."

Everything she saw Rapinoe put through was bad, Dunn said in a 2020 round table organized by *Bleacher Report*: "But to me, I was thinking 'they could rip up my contract.' So I thought I was actually going to get it much worse. And I remember telling her, it hurts me to my core that I'm going to stand, but I'm supportive."

Knowing how tangible that fear is only serves to highlight the courage of those who decided to kneel anyway—when they didn't have the protection of celebrity that Rapinoe had. The Super Bowl that followed the 2017 season was played in Minneapolis, and the people in the region affected by the killing of Philando Castile in 2016 took advantage by hosting a week of activism for the fans and worldwide media in attendance. One of the organizers was a then-sophomore at Minneapolis's Augsburg University, a Black woman named Olivia House—a soccer player who had kneeled before her team's games all season.

House said that Kaepernick had confirmed her understanding of how powerful a platform sports provided. Seeing Rapinoe take a knee in support of Kaepernick and his cause, and the reasons that she stated for doing it, nudged her to action.

"It kind of lit a fire in me," she said the week of the Super Bowl. "I said, 'Yeah, that's why I'm doing this.'"

House's experience in kneeling was similar to Rapinoe's: Throughout the season, she was usually the only player on either team kneeling. These solo protests in sports and leagues and on teams were the norm.

One of the most noticeable abstainers from the anthem and flag ritual in the NFL was Michael Bennett of the Seattle Seahawks. He always spoke supportively of Kaepernick, and he always chose to sit during the anthem—in 2016, when such protests began, and in 2017, when groups of players or even entire rosters chose a collective gesture in response to Donald Trump's "sons of bitches" condemnation.

Bennett had additional motivation in the 2017 season, after he described his assault by police officers in Las Vegas after attending the Floyd Mayweather–Conor McGregor bout in August of that year. After Bennett spoke out about the incident, the Las Vegas Police Department wrote to NFL commissioner Roger Goodell, asking that the league punish Bennett not just for making what the department claimed was a "false accusation" but, it hinted, for not saluting the flag or honoring the anthem. The letter to Goodell notes that the league "condone[s] Bennett's disrespect for our American Flag, and everything it symbolizes."

Goodell, for his part, issued a statement supporting and defending Bennett as someone who "represents the best of the NFL—a leader on his team and in his community." He did not punish him. The police department later exonerated itself of wrongdoing against Bennett after an internal investigation.

Even with a major city police department calling out the NFL as a whole over what it perceived as disrespect for America, Bennett was still largely by himself when it came time to make a gesture on the sidelines—with one teammate standing next to him with a hand on his shoulder.

That was in football, the sport where the protests of that era began, in a league comprising roughly 70 percent Black players. It's not hard, then, to grasp the sense of isolation that Bruce Maxwell experienced in baseball, a sport whose percentage of Black American players (a crucial distinction from its strong Afro-Latino representation over the last four decades) stays in the single digits: still just 7 percent on Opening Day of the 2021 season.

Baseball might like to reignite interest among Black fans, but reactions like the one Maxwell faced damage its reputation. Without a more open-armed embrace of Black participants, supporters, and visibility in any way, that reputation is well on its way toward plummeting to NASCAR levels of interest from Black American viewers. In NASCAR's defense, the auto sport's leadership put considerable effort into changing its image as being virulently anti-Black in its presentation and imagery, which centered around a flag—not the American flag but the Confederate battle flag, popular across the sport for decades and fiercely protected by its base.

When the sport's lone Black racer in its top tier of competition in 2020, Bubba Wallace, began openly supporting Black Lives Matter and the post-Floyd social justice movement, NASCAR supported him by banning the Confederate flag at all its races, events, and venues. Not long after that, a noose was found in Wallace's garage at the legendary Talladega Superspeedway. That incident prompted a federal investigation and a solidarity march on the track by the other drivers, with Wallace in his car. The drivers also supported the ban on Confederate flags. A large segment of fans, however, tried to defy the ban as often as possible for the rest of the season, performing their own acts of rebellion and displays of allegiance to a different flag than the one most habitually defended by Americans.

Flags and anthems show no signs of being even partly or minimally removed from sports at any level or of being used as outward symbols of demands for oaths of loyalty to the country. Thus, they show no signs of being unavailable to demonstrators as platforms for protest by athletes or any other participants. There have been very few attempts to break the anthem-flag tradition at the start of sports games. The Dallas Mavericks organization reversed its decision to stop playing the anthem before games in the 2020–21 season after conservative media outlets led an outcry against it. There have been more attempts to make playing the anthem mandatory (bills introduced by legislatures in Texas and Wisconsin in 2021).

The hypocritical use of a flag as a weapon against those looking to exercise their legal rights to achieve change and reform in the U.S. stands in direct contrast to the unity and humility that the critics of anthem protests profess the pregame ritual is meant to inspire.

The most obvious and recent example of the flag's use as a weapon in spite—not support—of democratic freedoms was the images from the violent attempted coup at the U.S. Capitol building in Washington, D.C., on January 6, 2021. Rioters were captured beating police officers and other members of law enforcement with flagpoles with American flags attached. One trespasser walked the halls of Congress with an enormous Confederate flag. All over the Capitol grounds and all over the city were bastardized versions of the American flag, including the white, black, and blue "Blue Lives Matter" flags, mocking and signifying their bearers' rejection of the concept of Black Lives Matter, the very issue that Kaepernick was illuminating by kneeling.

That stands as only the most recent example. The infamous photo of a white opponent of Boston's school busing program lunging at a Black lawyer with a flag pole carrying the American flag brandished like a pike—a photo that won a Pulitzer Prize and would later be featured in the opening credits of the Spike Lee movie *School Daze*—was taken in 1976, not even a decade after Smith and Carlos raised their fists in Mexico City.

5

JUSTICE LEAGUE

The WNBA Takes the Lead

Athletes spanning the sports world at every level reacted strongly and publicly to the shooting deaths of Alton Sterling and Philando Castile by police in July 2016. Colin Kaepernick, of course, was among them, and so was LeBron James.

The first athletes to act were members of the Minnesota Lynx, and the rest of the players in the Women's National Basketball Association (WNBA) immediately followed. The players, their teams, and—sometimes reluctantly—the league kept up the pace for the next several years. They did more than move along with the movement. Far more often, they were at the head of the movement.

Kaepernick posted an Instagram message about the murder of Sterling ("This is what lynchings look like in 2016!") on July 6 and tweeted about Castile's slaying ("We are under attack! It's clear as day!") the next day. On July 9, the Lynx took the court in Minneapolis wearing black T-shirts that read on the front, "Change starts with us. Justice & accountability." On the back were Sterling's and Castile's names and "Black Lives Matter." Castile had been shot in nearby Falcon Heights, by officer Jeronimo Yanez of the City of St. Anthony police department.

(Also on the back of the shirts was the emblem of the Dallas Police Department—Dallas officers had been attacked by a sniper at a march against police brutality after the killings of Castile and Sterling, and four officers had been killed before the gunman was caught and slain by police later that night.)

This display was nearly two months before Kaepernick was first witnessed sitting out the national anthem in Santa Clara (although, remember, he apparently had already sat in previous exhibition games). The Lynx's gesture did not go overlooked—"underplayed" might describe it better—and despite the courage that it took for the players to do it, it didn't pack the cultural punch that the act of a well-known National Football League (NFL) quarterback did.

It can never be said, though, that it wasn't noticed. The Minneapolis police department certainly noticed it.

Several of the off-duty officers who worked security at the arena for that game saw the T-shirts and walked off their jobs. They did so with the full support of the president of the city police union, the Police Officers Federation of Minneapolis—Lt. Bob Kroll. His words, history, and actions would come under scrutiny some four years later, when Derek Chauvin and three of his colleagues killed George Floyd. To the women's basketball players demanding justice for a local resident who had been killed on camera by an officer with no apparent provocation, Kroll leveled accusations of "rushing to judgment before the facts are in."

Kroll did not address whether Yanez had rushed to judgment with Castile. Maya Moore of the Lynx, meanwhile, made it clear that this was not a rushed, poorly thought-out act, with hastily chosen words devoid of facts.

"We as a nation can decide to stand up for what is right, no matter your race, background, or social status," she said after the game. "It is time that we take a deep look at our ability to be compassionate and empathetic to those suffering from the problems that are deep within our society. Again, this is a human issue, and we need to speak out for change together."

It wasn't clear yet whether the week's collective events represented a breaking point for the patience of the people who wanted an end to the atrocities by the police and the culture that had cultivated them. From the active athletes' perspectives, things had not yet progressed beyond social media posts, published interviews, and posted statements. The ESPYS ceremony during which LeBron James, Chris Paul, Dwyane Wade, and Carmelo Anthony would make their public appeal was still several days away.

The great exception was the WNBA teams. The players committed to keeping the momentum brought by the Lynx protest going. They established themselves as the leaders that other athletes and other sports followed. They drew up a blueprint that others relied on, and even copied. They studied the words and actions of other athletes in other sports and adapted the most effective ones to their own individual and collective goals. They set standards that other leagues and players realized were not impossible and indeed were very much worth reaching. They exemplified "allyship" when other athletes only gestured toward it. They put their leaders' feet to the fire and nudged them out the door, if necessary. Their biggest stars, like Moore, stepped to the forefront—and their role players, such as Natasha Cloud, became stars in the movement right next to them. Several players made their marks without even playing.

And they changed the course of American political history—to the point where they directly helped flip control of two branches of the federal government. At the same time, and for the same reasons, they rewrote the rules on player empowerment when they drove out the most objectionable owner in league history and replaced her with one of the players from her former team.

Moore's name continually surfaced throughout this period of upheaval. Every time, it was for the best of reasons, even when the four-time champion, six-time All-Star, two-time Olympic gold medalist, and former league Most Valuable Player (MVP) was away from the team, the league, and the sport entirely. She fit the description of the league's golden age of activism perfectly: She wasn't necessarily overlooked or unnoticed, but she genuinely deserved as much notice, if not more, than any other athletic figure of our time. Kaepernick, for obvious reasons, will likely never be depicted as the NFL's mascot. If Moore eventually became the face of the WNBA, though, who could argue? In fact, who could argue against rewarding her this way sooner rather than later?

Moore would, indeed, soon step into an arena even larger than the one in which she wore a black T-shirt in July 2016. But there in Minneapolis, the stage was large enough. Her status as a league MVP made her an ideal spokesperson for her teammates. Significantly, she had the backing of all her teammates, and they all took part in the action equally—she was joined in her initial comments that night by Seimone Augustus, Rebekkah Brunson, and Lindsay Whalen.

This was not another case of Black players stepping to the forefront with direct engagement while white players rested a hand on their shoulder. White WNBA players wore the T-shirts with their Black teammates and stood with them on the court, in the locker room, in front of reporters, and in photos. They took the same level of heat, including the angry reaction from the police and those who support the police. There was no real norm for this level of protest yet—the norm that would later be established in the few sports where protests took place saw white players, no matter their level of fame, accomplishment, or celebrity, stay on the periphery while Black players lived in the eye of the storm. When other WNBA teams joined the Lynx and mimicked their tactics, all players took part again.

The contrast across sports was sharp in Seattle. A few months later, Megan Rapinoe's teammates on the National Women's Soccer League's (NWSL's) Reign, and around the league, left her to protest by herself and face the wrath of the league, the governing body, and all the critics. On the WNBA's Storm, Sue Bird, one of the greatest players in league history and one of the faces of the sport, proved to also be one of the faces of the protest. Bird and Rapinoe began dating sometime the following year and became one of sport's most visible and vocal couples in the ensuing years as the various protest movements began to spread. Bird, however, was always part of a united front of players on her team and in her sport, signaling that the WNBA teams were a unit. It took far longer for Rapinoe to see that same level of support around her sport at any level.

The first team to extend the Lynx's protest was the New York Liberty; the day after the Lynx protest, Liberty players donned black T-shirts with "Black Lives Matter" messages as well, posted their messages all over social media, and conducted a "media blackout"—they only spoke about the social issues at hand to reporters, nothing game-related or even consequence-related. The latter was a heated topic, considering the reaction of the Minneapolis officers and considering that the league office itself could punish the players at any time. The Liberty's management—in particular team president and Basketball Hall of Famer Isiah Thomas—gave the players their full support to do what they believed was necessary. Liberty player Tanisha Wright, who was also the vice president of the Women's National Basketball Players Association (WNBPA), took the lead in connecting with players around the league, advising them and checking the temperature in their locker rooms and in their interactions with management. By and large, the players and team executives were on the same page. Locker rooms were united, regardless of race and regardless of status as an All-Star or fringe player.

"We were the majority, in a situation where we are never the majority. We are always the minority," Wright, speaking to the *Sporting News* in 2018, said of the Black WNBA players, who make up 80 percent of the rosters from year to year. "So it was interesting and awesome to see [the white players] really with us and really be an ally in that situation. We were fortunate, to be honest, in terms of having people support us."

They soon found out who supported them and who did not. About two weeks after the protests began, the WNBA and league president Lisa Borders—the chief executive, in the years before that position's title was changed to "commissioner"—fined three teams $5,000 each and their players $500 each, citing uniform violations when the players took the court in black warmup T-shirts before games.

The players' response: Three more teams wore the black warmups on the floor for their next games, and they blasted the fines on their social media accounts. One of the most widely circulated came from the Storm, posted this time by Breanna Stewart, with a Martin Luther King Jr. quote ("There comes a time when silence is betrayal") and "We Will Not Be Silenced" in hashtag form. Driving home the message of full unity across racial lines—Stewart is white.

National Basketball Association (NBA) players, in the middle of their off-season, leaped to their WNBA counterparts' defense. So did Stewart's former college coach, Hall of Fame University of Connecticut coach Geno Auriemma. So did team executives, including Thomas. So did alternately famous and infamous civil rights activist the Rev. Al Sharpton, who announced that his New York–based National Action Network would pay the players' fines.

The WNBA office buckled a day later. "Appreciate our players expressing themselves on matters important to them. Rescinding imposed fines to show them even more support," Borders tweeted, in a dazzling display of wordsmanship. The fence that the league had straddled by justifying the discipline as related to a uniform violation had collapsed under it. The fines, in fact, gave the impression that the league did not actually appreciate the players' expressing themselves, nor did they indicate that it was supporting them.

In a sense, the template was set. The players were leading, and the league was following, and not always succeeding in staying out of the way. Borders herself was not hurt by the misstep on the fines; she remained president for two more years and left on good terms after the 2018 season to join the workplace advocacy organization Time's Up. The protests took place during her first season in charge. To her credit, the league continued its upward arc in exposure and popularity.

The arc of player activism continued upward as well.

Kaepernick began his protests in August 2016, with a smattering of NFL players joining in various forms. The WNBA regular season was heading toward its conclusion. In a September game, all the players on the New York Liberty and the Phoenix Mercury teams locked arms as they stood for the national anthem. The next night, the entire Indiana Fever team and two Mercury players kneeled during the anthem. That demonstration featured all three teams that had been fined by the league earlier in the summer.

The 2017 season witnessed the players' continued awareness and willingness to take stands. In August of that season, a rally by white supremacists, including neo-Nazis and Confederate sympathizers, in Charlottesville, Virginia, devolved into violent attacks on counter-protestors, culminating with a man plowing his car into a crowd and killing resister Heather Heyer. The police in large part stood by and did nothing or protected the white supremacists. President Donald Trump reacted in a speech soon afterward by defending the rights of the white supremacists, saying that there were "very fine people on both sides" and attempting to assign part of the blame for the rioting to the victims.

Again, the WNBA players took the initiative, even while most of the other major sports leagues seasons were underway in one form or another. (The NFL exhibition season was underway, but Kaepernick was not part of it.) Five teams—again including the Storm and the Lynx—linked arms during the playing of the anthem before games over the next several days.

When the league finals between the Minnesota Lynx and the Los Angeles Sparks began in Minneapolis in late September 2017, the sports world was grappling with Trump's castigation of Kaepernick and fellow NFL protesters in his Alabama campaign speech. The NFL players' (and, in many cases, teams') reactions are well documented—they kneeled in unison, or showed support for kneeling teammates, or made decisions about whether to take the field during the playing of the anthem, which were sporadically followed. The rationale for the NFL teams' avoiding the anthem's playing altogether was exactly that: to avoid an unpredictable player action or reaction.

Before Game 1 of those WNBA finals, the Lynx players stood at the free-throw line with arms linked and heads lowered. The Sparks players stayed in their locker room and did not take the court until the anthem had ended. Both teams repeated their choices for the first four games; the Sparks stayed on the court for the fifth and final game, with the Lynx still linking arms.

The Lynx, like the teams earlier in the year and the season before, linked arms with a purpose. The Sparks stayed off the court with the same purpose. This was now the second season in which they remained solid in their convictions. The messages in every other sport were scrambled. That wasn't the case in this one.

As Borders, the league president, told reporters before the first game of the finals, "Our players are some of the most socially conscious that you will ever find. You have seen that in the years before I got here, and I'm sure it will continue in the future."

The Lynx won that 2017 championship, the franchise's fourth and Moore's fourth in a seven-year span. She returned in 2018 and was an All-Star again, but the Lynx couldn't repeat as champion. The following year, 2019, it was Moore who chose not to repeat—at age twenty-eight, after eight seasons, she announced that she was taking a sabbatical to concentrate on her family and her Christian ministry. In her announcement, she said, "The success that I've been a part of in basketball truly blows my mind every time I think about it. But the main way I measure success in life is something I don't often get to emphasize explicitly through pro ball. I measure success by asking, 'Am I living out my purpose?'"

Moore ended up manifesting that purpose by working to free Jonathan Irons, who had been in state prison in Missouri since 1998, serving a fifty-year sentence for a crime committed when he was sixteen. Irons and others had insisted that he was wrongly convicted on charges of burglary and assault with a deadly weapon. Her family factored into her quest here, as well—she had spent part of her childhood in the area where Irons was imprisoned, and her relatives knew him and believed that he was innocent and that the judicial system had done him terribly wrong. Not long before beginning her college career at the University of Connecticut, Moore joined her family on their visit to the prison and met Irons for the first time. From then on, throughout her college and professional life, she stayed in touch with him and took on his fight for exoneration.

Moore didn't limit her departure from the sport to a year; she would stay away for the 2020 and 2021 seasons as well. Her efforts paid off in July 2020, when Irons's conviction was overturned and he was freed from prison; the video that she shot of his release and her and his supporters greeting him went viral immediately. Soon afterward, Moore and Irons announced that they had gotten married. Moore kept her activism on behalf of criminal justice reform going after his release and their marriage.

In her absence, Moore's legend grew—as a player whose brilliance was missed, but even more so as a person who sacrificed the prime of her career and the comfortable life that it brought to go even further toward her goals than she had as an athlete in the spotlight. Even as Kaepernick, James, the Milwaukee Bucks players, and her WNBA teammates were lauded for their outspokenness in the years following the advent of the police brutality protests, Moore's advocates in and around the WNBA never took a break from reminding all of the lengths Moore had gone to for her cause. Everything she did reflected well on the league that she had walked away from and on the players with whom she no longer played.

The 2020 season, meanwhile, elevated WNBA players once again. As a league, they managed to shine brightest during one of the bleakest stretches of time in American history, by far the bleakest of the twenty-first century.

The timing of the WNBA season gave the league—under commissioner Cathy Engelbert, in office for her first full season—a semblance of an advantage over the other major sports in plotting out a schedule and a maintenance plan in the middle of the COVID-19 pandemic that struck in March 2020. The NBA, the National Hockey League (NHL), and the National Collegiate Athletic Association (NCAA) basketball seasons came to abrupt halts; Major League Baseball (MLB) cut off spring training and delayed and reduced the season; and the Olympic Games were postponed for a year. The WNBA shifted to a bubble format that the NBA and the NHL also adopted. Because the WNBA season didn't start until summer, the league had a chance to reorganize its season before play started, and players had an opportunity to decide how they would approach the unusual conditions that the burgeoning pandemic would bring before play started. The WNBA also gave players the option to sit out the season, primarily for health reasons. Those determinations were clumsy at times, as it turned out, as former MVP and centerpiece of the reigning league champion Washington Mystics, Elena Delle Donne, had to wait an uncomfortable amount of time to have her opt-out request approved.

The players, meanwhile, put a twist on the opt-out choice, one that was discussed by NBA players about their eventual return, but that was brought out in full form in the women's league: Players began declaring their decision to sit out the year to dedicate their time to advocacy and activism. The most notable were Renee Montgomery of the Atlanta Dream and Cloud of the Washington Mystics. Nneka Ogwumike of the Sparks considered opting out for the same reasons but decided to play only when, in her role as president of the WNBPA, she had secured promises of commitment to social justice from the league.

The players were making these decisions in June, with the season approaching in July, and with what had transpired at the end of May weighing on their minds: Floyd's killing. The choice was exacerbated by another unjustifiable police killing, the shooting death of twenty-six-year-old Breonna Taylor in her home late at night by Louisville, Kentucky, officers serving a warrant on somebody else. The Taylor incident was starting to draw more attention as the entire law enforcement system was brought to account in the aftermath of Floyd's murder. Such players as Montgomery and Cloud were engaged in the protests—Cloud led a Black Lives Matter march in Washington with her NBA counterpart, the Washington Wizards' Bradley Beal—but their insistence that Taylor not be lost in the coverage of their own advocacy was embraced by their WNBA colleagues.

That insistence led to the most outward show of support for the cause by any group of athletes during the year of reckoning. When the season began in the bubble in July, the name and image of Taylor were hung in the arena, and her name was printed on the jersey of every player, for every game, through the end of the finals. Their warmup shirts bore the phrase "Say Her Name."

Cloud and Montgomery, meanwhile, made themselves heard without ever stepping on the court in 2020.

One of the landmark shifts that emerged from the players' activism for civic change was the opening of NBA arenas—and, eventually, playing facilities across the major sports leagues—for voting, either registration, balloting, or both. Cloud can take great credit for that initiative, with her constant push to prioritize voting in the 2020 general elections. She had begun advocating for that even before the league's players walked out after the Jacob Blake killing in August, but the movement accelerated afterward. Washington agreed to open the downtown arena that was home to the Wizards and the NHL's Capitals and the baseball stadium for the then-defending World Series champion Nationals.

Cloud decided that wasn't good enough. The Mystics' home building, the Entertainment and Sports Arena, was located in one of the most notoriously neglected neighborhoods in the city, one that had held that distinction for generations—Ward 8, in the southeast quadrant of Washington, D.C. The arena, still fairly new, was also the Wizards' practice facility, and, to its credit, the city had targeted it as a destination to help uplift the area. It was also ten to fifteen minutes, in good traffic, from the baseball and soccer stadiums on the city's heavily developing waterfront, but still seemingly millions of miles away from them in allure. The city had not included the arena in its plans for voting locations.

Cloud addressed the issue on her social media accounts: "How can we make this happen? When we moved into SE we promised this community we would be a part of the solution. Let's not just talk about it . . . let's be about it."

Her pressure swayed the decision makers: Within days, the city added the arena in the southeast quadrant to its voting locations, granting access to democracy to a population who otherwise would have struggled to get it.

Montgomery was simultaneously pushing hard for voter registration and access in Atlanta and across Georgia, with the greatest of rewards at stake. Georgia was all but certain to be a major determining factor in the presidential race between Trump, the incumbent, and the Democratic challenger, Joe Biden. The state's governor and legislature had openly engaged in voter suppression to tilt results over the years. The pandemic was sure to affect turnout, and access to voting alternatives was being blocked and contested to keep Black voters away. Finally, both of Georgia's Senate seats were being contested—both held by Republicans, one of whom was Kelly Loeffler, who had been appointed to her seat after the resignation of her predecessor and was now running for the first time for a full term.

Loeffler was also a co-owner of Montgomery's team, the Atlanta Dream. And she had spent considerable time since the growth of the social justice movement that year trashing athletes—including players in her own league and on her own team—for supporting the Black Lives Matter movement.

Loeffler did more than castigate them in speeches, interviews, and social media. She wrote to Engelbert, the commissioner, demanding that the league reverse course on plans to print "Black Lives Matter" on the court in the bubble when the season began.

"The truth is, we need less—not more politics in sports," her letter reads, in part. "In a time when polarizing politics is as divisive as ever, sports has the power to be a unifying antidote. And now more than ever, we should be united in our goal to remove politics from sports."

Included in the letter, however, is a painfully racist and lie-filled characterization of the movement, which she claims "has advocated for the defunding of police, called for the removal of Jesus from churches and the disruption of the nuclear family structure, harbored anti-Semitic views, and promoted violence and destruction across the country. I believe it is totally misaligned with the values and goals of the WNBA and the Atlanta Dream, where we support tolerance and inclusion."

The players, to a person, immediately demanded that Loeffler be expelled as co-owner, knowing that such a move was not unprecedented in the sport after the NBA in 2014 had forced Donald Sterling to sell the Los Angeles Clippers and banned him for life for his unapologetically racist behavior.

The players association's plea was the most succinct: a tweet that read, "E-N-O-U-G-H! O-U-T!"

The WNBA did not put Loeffler out. It tread lightly, pointing out that she was not a team governor, that the league was still committed to the Black Lives Matter movement and to player activism, and that if new ownership came in, they would be welcome. It steered away from condemning Loeffler.

The players' response, almost immediately after that, was to coordinate to get Loeffler voted out of the Senate. Not just to campaign against her generally, though—they researched the candidates, found which one fit their preferences, and threw their support into that likely general election candidate. That opponent, far behind Loeffler in the polls at the time, was Rev. Raphael Warnock, the pastor of Atlanta's venerable Ebenezer Baptist Church.

Again, the stakes went beyond getting rid of an objectionable owner, stripping her of her political power, or both. Their activism went beyond speaking against Loeffler and into throwing their platform behind their preferred alternative and opening polls to allow voters a chance to participate. If Georgia could put Democrats into the two Senate seats, the Democratic party would likely win the Senate and regain the balance of power, potentially for a new Democratic president and in concert with a majority in the House of Representatives.

Almost immediately after the tepid response by the league office, more photos of players began to blanket the social universe—of players on every team, from coast to coast, Atlanta and everywhere else, wearing "Vote Warnock" shirts. They posed for them in their arenas and in the streets, on the court during warmups, and afterward in interviews. It was a pleasant surprise voting bloc for Warnock, who eagerly embraced it.

Warnock's election went into a runoff with Loeffler after the November results came back. The January runoff—January 5, to be exact, the day before the Capitol insurrection—resulted in a Warnock victory, a new balance of power in the Senate, and the end of Loeffler's brief tenure in Congress.

The WNBA still waited for the now-private citizen to be eased out by other circumstances. In February, they were announced: The Dream had been sold to a group of real estate magnates and other investors. Loeffler, an ex-U.S. Senator, was now also an ex-WNBA team owner.

One of the investors, the person who brought the purchasing group together, was one of the players who had opted out of the season to pursue social advocacy and advance a movement that Loeffler had labeled as "totally misaligned with the values and goals" of the league.

The investor was Montgomery of the Atlanta Dream.

6

PETER NORMAN, CHRIS LONG, AND GREGG POPOVICH

White Allies

Black athletes have always had to clear a substantial barrier when making their statements to the public—that the public, which is still predominantly white, even as the demographics advance toward nonwhite people becoming the majority in the United States, cannot relate to them and their cause.

Colin Kaepernick's earliest opponents proved the salience of that racial disconnect, latching on to his parentage and who raised him as proof that he had no business protesting oppression because he could not possibly be oppressed. Not so much because he was due a salary of some $12 million in the 2016 season, but because he was biracial—a white mother and a Black father—and was raised by white adoptive parents a few levels above the wrenching poverty that's become a staple of the stereotypical Black athlete narrative.

Generally speaking, the Black members of the public get the point of the athletes' demonstrations, even when they know how skewed the earnings and lifestyle of professional athletes are. Dr. Glenn Bracey, a sociology professor at Villanova who studies critical race theory and social movements, including those in sports, gave the phenomenon a name. "We're all connected," he told the *Sporting News*. "In political science, they call it 'linked fate': for African-Americans in particular, that what happens to one happens to us all."

From the perspective of the players putting themselves on the record on the behalf of others, Black people seem to recognize the struggle even in those who are a few degrees removed from it— because they never are completely removed from it.

"We automatically think of people that are close to us in those positions, and that's where the hurt comes from," said Tanisha Wright, the former Women's National Basketball Association (WNBA) player who participated in the protests against police brutality in 2016, in an interview with the *Sporting News*. "That's where the pain comes from, that's where the conversations come from, because we know."

Explaining that to white teammates who either genuinely want to understand or are demanding explanations for ideas and motivations that are beyond their experience can be an extra burden for Black athletes who are trying to win support—including from their own teammates. Basketball Hall of Famer Oscar Robertson struggled to convey that to his teammates and coaches at the University of Cincinnati during his painful interactions with racism on a road trip to Texas. When Elgin Baylor faced the Jim Crow conditions in Charleston, West Virginia, in his rookie year and refused to suit up for the then-Minneapolis Lakers' game there, his teammate Rod Hundley—immortalized as "Hot Rod" as a college star in Charleston and in the National Basketball Association (NBA) as a player and later a broadcaster—tried to convince him to play anyway. The two were friends and respected each other, but in Terry Pluto's oral history of the NBA's early years, *Tall Tales*, Hundley admits that he didn't understand how badly Baylor was hurt by the treatment. "Rod, I'm a human being, too. All I want to do is to be treated like a human being," Hundley recalls Baylor telling him, adding, "It was then that I could begin to feel his pain." Hundley ended up telling the game's sponsors as much . . . and the sponsors still demanded that the NBA punish Baylor.

Private educations like that, though, tend to be preferable to public ones—as future Hall of Fame quarterback Drew Brees learned in the off-season before the 2020 season. Brees was one of many white National Football League (NFL) players who criticized Kaepernick's 2016 protests, but as the years passed and Brees continued to pile up NFL records and lead his New Orleans Saints into contention, his words were largely forgotten. Then, as the protests in the wake of George Floyd's killing picked up speed, he added fresh salt to the wound in a video interview with the Yahoo! Finance website. "I will never agree with anybody disrespecting the flag of the United States of America or our country," he said, adding that what mattered to him during such protests were his grandparents and other relatives who had fought in previous wars. The implication was two-fold, at least: firstly, that Kaepernick's protests were not against the brutal mistreatment of Black citizens but about turning his back on his country, and secondly, that Brees's family's sacrifice in the military was important, but those of the families of Black people, including his own teammates, were all but nonexistent.

The harshest condemnation of Brees's words came from his own Black teammates. Two of them, former wide receiver Marques Colston and safety Malcolm Jenkins, each called their quarterback "part of the problem." Wide receiver Emmanuel Sanders point-blank called him "ignorant." Louisianians who had taken to the streets to protest Floyd's killing began to acknowledge the blind spots of the star universally acknowledged as a franchise savior and a hero of the recovery of New Orleans after Hurricane Katrina. "Fuck Drew Brees!" marchers were caught on video chanting as they marched.

Brees tried twice to clean up the mess with posted apologies—or attempts at apologies. The team resumed its preparation for the pandemic season, played well, and reached the play-offs again, and Brees retired a year later after a twenty-year career. His patronizing, privileged tone as that career neared the finish line will be part of his legacy.

Proving their own vulnerability to their teammates is a hurdle that activist athletes would rather not have to clear. It's also something about which those activists tend to have low expectations. Support from white teammates, colleagues, other athletes, coaches, staffers, executives, administrators, owners, and commissioners can be invaluable. But one would assume that the decision to venture into the storm of public protest is made without the assurance that any, never mind just a handful or the majority of, white athletes in their circle will stand with them.

Roughly 80 percent of the WNBA's players are Black, but when they began protesting the deaths of Philando Castile, Alton Sterling, and others in 2016, white players spoke and wore the messages that their Black teammates did. In 2020, when players wore Breonna Taylor's name on their jerseys and modeled "Vote Warnock" shirts, they *all* wore them. More often than not, when they linked arms, kneeled, or walked off the court during the playing of "The Star-Spangled Banner," they did it together.

The history of white allies back in the early days of sports, integration, and the grip of turn-of-the-twentieth-century white supremacy is fairly slim. Jack Johnson and Paul Robeson did not tend to have white advocates in their fields running interference for them, taking up their cause as they tried to knock down the societal barriers in front of them and their people. Jesse Owens and Joe Louis had Americans rallying to their sides when they were in direct competition with the athletic symbols of Nazi Germany—but even when positive relationships formed that didn't clearly cause them harm, neither man had anyone in their circles who could be called an ally. A durable legend has formed around Pee Wee Reese and his years as a teammate of Jackie Robinson with the Dodgers, a legend that everybody recognizes on sight by now: Reese putting an arm around Robinson on the field during a road game as boos and slurs rained down on them from the stands. Fueled by scattered and somewhat unreliable eyewitness accounts years after the fact, it is generally considered an urban legend now, debunked by, among many others, none other than Robinson's widow, Rachel. Reese and Robinson became lifelong friends, and their bond was a case of opposites overlooking their differences due to Reese's Southern upbringing. But the embellishment of the supposed arm-around-the-shoulder moment likely wasn't necessary or particularly instructive.

The white allyship that did the best job of breaking the mold and signifying an advance in the storyline was the one offered by Australian sprinter Peter Norman. He was the silver medalist in the 200-meter final at the 1968 Olympics (he nipped John Carlos at the wire in a breathtaking race that still thrills upon viewing all these years later) and occupier of the silver-medal position on the podium in Mexico City. He stood at attention, facing the flag as Carlos and Tommie Smith raised their fists—but he wore an Olympic Project for Human Rights (OPHR) pin on his team jacket. He had asked the two about the project while they were all preparing to go to the medals stand; there probably wasn't much he didn't know about it by then, after more than a year of publicity about the movement and the speculation about a boycott and then about an athlete protest. They either offered him the pin or he asked for one—it depends on who tells the story. But he wore it, and that act became an international story, just as the protest itself did.

The scorn heaped upon Norman by some of his fellow Australians, including some in the country's Olympic governing body, after his return home from the Games has become common knowledge. Olympic officials have always denied any animosity toward him—but they did have to go to great lengths again to smooth over drama of their own creation in 2000 when Norman had no significant role in the Sydney Games. There was brief speculation that he was under consideration to light the Olympic flame, or at least to be part of the relay at the ceremony, but he was not even *at* the ceremony, as neither the Australian nor International Olympic committees had invited him. Norman was welcomed, however, at the dedication of the statue of Smith and Carlos at San José State University in 2003—he was embraced by the crowd and by Smith, Carlos, and Dr. Harry Edwards. When Norman died in 2006, Smith and Carlos traveled to Australia to be his pallbearers.

Norman is in many ways the gold standard for white athletes who follow their conscience and stand with Black athletes in their struggle. He is often presented as "the forgotten man" in the Mexico City protest—but it has been suggested so often over the decades that it's made it impossible to forget his role, the way that "underrated" players are mentioned so often that they negate the meaning of the word. Most white athletes who choose to support their Black teammates who take up the mantle of advocacy are compared to him in one way or another.

The white players in the WNBA are. So are the white players who have stood with the Kaepernicks and the other NFL players who have kneeled, sat, raised a fist, or otherwise displayed their resistance. One of the very first to do that in the NFL, in 2017, was the Seahawks' Justin Britt, who stood next to teammate Michael Bennett as he sat on the sidelines during the national anthem and put a hand on his shoulder in support. Kicker Steven Hauschka, a former Seahawks teammate of Bennett, supported him from afar after Hauschka signed with the Bills in 2017; he told the *Buffalo News* that year, "I think a lot of white people don't understand it and are afraid to be involved. . . . And I think it's important for white people to see there is inequality everywhere in the country right now, and in the world."

A month before, during the exhibition season, Seth DeValve joined eleven of his Cleveland Browns teammates in kneeling before a game, the first white player to take a knee in the NFL. When the season began and demonstrations spread in the wake of Donald Trump's "sons of bitches" comment, most white players passed on kneeling or raising fists—but Philadelphia Eagles defensive end

Chris Long very publicly stood next to then-teammate Malcolm Jenkins (the same player who later played in New Orleans and lashed out at Brees's condemnation of Kaepernick). As Jenkins raised his fist, as he and many others had that year and the season before, Long put an arm around him. The two continued that throughout the season—which ended with an Eagles Super Bowl victory. Long began speaking out when asked to, joining Jenkins as one of the most outspoken players on racial oppression and inequality on the team.

As it turned out, Long—who had always been considered a valuable, mature, cohesive locker-room presence throughout his career to that point—was moved to show on-field support for Jenkins by Bennett. The Seahawks player who had begun sitting during the anthem, and who had told of his violent, abusive treatment by the Las Vegas police, said in an interview with ESPN.com:

> I honestly believe that it would take a white player to really get things changed. When somebody from the other side understands and they step up and they speak about it, it would change the whole conversation because you bring somebody who doesn't really have to be part of the conversation to make themselves vulnerable in front of it. I think when that happens things will really take a big jump.

Teammate Britt began supporting Bennett after that. Long's gesture on the Eagles' sideline soon followed. "Obviously, it's changed the dynamic of the whole conversation," Jenkins said.

The true effectiveness of the league-wide protest by players that season after Trump's insulting comments came from the exponential growth in the number of white teammates participating. They still declined to kneel along with the Black players, or raise their fists, but the images of the hands and arms on the shoulders drove home the precise point that Bennett, Jenkins, and others were making. It definitely was a noticeable shift from the wave of white players who went as far as threatening Kaepernick a year earlier; from the teammates who stoically stood separately from the Black players on the sideline, sometimes at attention with hands over hearts; from the ones who volunteered to carry the American flags onto the field for introductions; and from the likes of Alejandro Villanueva, who decided to stand in the stadium tunnel for the playing of the anthem while his Steelers teammates held to their pledge to stay in the locker room. Even some of the observers who supported him and attributed his choice to his years in the military saw his move as at least a little performative.

Those players also found a window to show support where they previously had stayed aggressively neutral. The list of marquee white players who supported their teammates in that 2017 season—after they had previously made a point of not committing to Kaepernick's cause during the 2016 season, when he was in so much of the country's crosshairs—was long. It clearly did not include Brees, but it did include Tom Brady, Aaron Rodgers, Eli Manning, J. J. Watt, Luke Kuechly, Ben Roethlisberger, Andrew Luck, Rob Gronkowski, Clay Matthews, and a host of others. But many of those players put themselves at least on the perimeter of those crosshairs by placing their hands on the shoulders of their teammates. In Foxborough, Massachusetts, where Devin McCourty, Martellus Bennett, and several other Black players had been raising their fists during the anthem, Brady joined his teammates in standing and linking arms—as fans showered the players with the boos that they had previously reserved for the kneeling protestors. The same was the case for Rodgers at Green Bay's Lambeau Field. At a prime-time game in the suburbs of Washington, players for both Washington and Oakland combined kneeling with linking arms—after both head coaches, Jay Gruden and Jack Del Rio, respectively, had previously stated clearly that they preferred not to see their players make any kind of gesture at all.

The stiffest test of the notion of cross-racial unity came later that season with the Houston Texans. In an ESPN story about a midseason meeting of the league's owners and the subject of player protests and Trump's incessant provocation, Texans owner Robert McNair was reported to have said of the defiant players, "We can't have the inmates running the prison."

Enraged players threatened to walk out of practice upon hearing the owner's comments. Star wide receiver DeAndre Hopkins did leave practice in anger. At the next week's game in Seattle, a good two-thirds of the players in uniform kneeled during the anthem, several others sat, and still others—including Watt, by far the most accomplished Texan and their most recognizable and beloved player—linked arms as they stood. Across the field, more Seattle Seahawks than in previous games chose to kneel, sit, link arms, or put hands on shoulders, partly in support of Bennett and partly in solidarity and empathy with the embittered Texans players.

Watt was the most prominent of the NFL players who enjoyed taking a personal role in the NFL's pregame rituals, usually racing onto the field while carrying a giant flag. While he never joined his teammates in 2016 in any form of protest, he still made the clear distinction between his method of honoring America and the rights of the players to exercise their freedoms. "I think everybody can do what they choose to do," Watt told reporters that season. "Everybody can form their own opinion on how they want to do it. That's just what we chose to do. Everybody's different, everybody has their own opinions, and that's what we chose to do."

In 2020, Watt was on the field with his teammates and the players on the Kansas City Chiefs when they made their linked-arms "Moment of Unity" gesture before the kickoff of their prime-time season opener. Several fans in the Chiefs' stadium, at less than full capacity because of COVID-19 restrictions, booed the gesture. Watt pointed out the obvious flaw in the logic of booing the gesture—harking back to his remark four years earlier about whether the rage at protesters was related to the perception of their patriotism.

"I don't fully understand that. There was no flag involved. There was nothing involved other than two teams coming together to show unity," Watt said.

Waves of Black people inside and outside the NFL, from players to fans to commenters and observers in various walks of life,
spoke up regarding the hypocrisy of the booing of a largely neutral
gesture that was distinct from the presence of the flag or the anthem. When Watt echoed this view, much of the public listened,
even if many still defended the fans' loud rejection of the gesture.
But if the observation of Bennett, Jenkins, and, even more pointedly, Megan Rapinoe—that the message of Black oppression needed to be passed along by white allies to be heard more widely and
clearly—had not already been proven by then, Watt took it further
toward being understood by all.

The support of white players in the social activism of the predominantly Black WNBA clarified the point further. Even more
clarity would be provided in the NBA in the years following the
events of 2016. By any measure, the NBA was still more mainstream
than the WNBA, more recognized by the public as one of the "major" leagues . . . and more regularly recognized as, in so many words,
the Blackest of the big-time sports. As the years progressed, while
white WNBA players bonded with their Black teammates, the faces
of the movement in the NBA were overwhelmingly Black—starting
at those ESPYS in the summer of 2016 with the speech by LeBron
James, Carmelo Anthony, Dwyane Wade, and Chris Paul.

The exception in the NBA was the head coaches, including the
most storied and famous ones. It was a huge exception and a notable asset. Coaches and managers in other leagues were not even
broadly noncommittal—they were overwhelmingly of the opinion
that players should stand during the anthem as a sign of respect for
America and stay away from the "distraction" of protests and the
reasons for them. The NFL was notorious for this—Gruden, Del
Rio, the Texans' Bill O'Brien, the Rams' Jeff Fisher, the Giants' Ben
McAdoo, the Panthers' Ron Rivera, and many others were openly
critical of the idea of players making any gestures at all, and they
almost unanimously conveyed the wishes and beliefs of their team
owners.

At the other end of that spectrum were NBA head coaches, including the Golden State Warriors' Steve Kerr, the San Antonio Spurs' Gregg Popovich, and Stan Van Gundy of the Detroit Pistons and, later, the New Orleans Pelicans.

They lent their voices and credibility to the players' cause from the beginning—or at least back to that contentious week in 2017, when Trump dragged the NFL player demonstrators. The president also went after Stephen Curry specifically and the Warriors generally when Curry (by then a perennial All-Star, a two-time Most Valuable Player [MVP], and a two-time league champion) pointedly said that he would not go to the White House for the traditional championship celebration while Trump was in office. "Stephen Curry is hesitating, therefore invitation is withdrawn!" Trump tweeted.

That was the genesis of James's famous "U bum!" Twitter rejoinder. It also inspired mocking from Kerr at a press conference during the Warriors' training camp: "He was going to break up with us before we broke up with him." He also threw Trump's cruel words about the previous month's deadly white supremacist rally in Charlottesville back in his face—asked whether the riot there had influenced his or the team's decision, Kerr said, "Nah, because there were very fine people on both sides."

During the same press conference, Kerr also recalled his White House visits and meetings with presidents after previous victories as a player for the Chicago Bulls and the San Antonio Spurs:

> I didn't necessarily agree with all of them, but it was an incredible honor to be in their presence. There was a respect for the office and also a respect from not only us, but from the president himself. I think we would, in normal times, very easily be able to set aside political differences, go visit and have a good time. But these are not ordinary times.

That same week, Popovich, of the five-time NBA champion Spurs, unloaded on the president. He had never held back his political opinions from the beginning of Trump's term of office, and he never slowed down through the end of his term and beyond. His reaction to the online outbursts against Curry, the Warriors, and the NFL's protesting players was utterly in character.

"It's like a sixth grader's going to have a party in his backyard, so he disinvites him. But again, I think the behavior, although it's disgusting, it's also comical," Popovich told reporters after a training camp practice.

The coach took his critique several steps beyond the comedic aspects of the president's behavior, though—he drilled down on white privilege, including his own, and the fact that willingness to be uncomfortable in the effort to disrupt a racist and corrupt system is essential:

> It's hard to sit down and decide that, yes, it's like you're at the 50-meter mark in a 100-meter dash. You've got that kind of a lead, yes, because you were born white. You have advantages that are systemically, culturally, psychologically rare. And they've been built up and cemented for hundreds of years. But many people can't look at it that way, because it's too difficult. It can't be something that's on their plate on a daily basis. People want to hold their position, people want their status quo, people don't want to give that up. Until it's given up, it's not going to be fixed.

The coach also said that day that his decision to speak out was not a matter of his having the platform of the NBA, of being a coach, of winning championships, or even so much of him being white. "I'm an individual, I live in this country, I have the right to say and think what I want," he said. The truth is, though, that all of those factors expand his platform farther than what any others might have, even global athletic figures like James and Curry.

Van Gundy was the head coach and president of the Detroit Pistons in 2016, when Kaepernick began demonstrating and when

Trump was elected. A day after Election Day, talking to reporters before a game in Phoenix, Van Gundy pulled no punches on the election winner and the people who put him in office:

> For our country to be where we are now, who took a guy who—I don't care what anyone says, I'm sure they have other reasons and maybe good reasons for voting for Donald Trump—but I don't think anybody can deny this guy is openly and brazenly racist and misogynistic and ethnic-centric, and say, "That's OK with us, we're going to vote for him anyway."

He was just warming up, as he moved on to the same territory where Kerr and Popovich were unafraid to go:

> I don't know how you go about it, if you're a person of color today or a Latino. Because white society just said to you, again—not like we haven't forever—but again, and emphatically, that I don't think you deserve equality. We don't think you deserve respect. And the same with women. That's what we say today, as a country. We should be ashamed for what we stand for as the United States today.

Ever since then—as the Pistons' coach, as a studio and game analyst for TNT, and then as the head coach of the New Orleans Pelicans—Van Gundy has kept up the public pressure on the hierarchy and the public support of the group most represented by the makeup of the league's players.

In the weeks following Trump's extended 2017 tirade against athletes, Van Gundy wrote an editorial for *TIME* magazine and described inviting scholar and author Michael Eric Dyson to speak to his Pistons players. (In similar fashion, Popovich invited John Carlos to speak to his team around the same time.) Van Gundy paraphrased Dyson's words in explaining his support of protesting athletes:

Nationalism, he said, is supporting your country no matter what, right or wrong. Patriotism, on the other hand, is caring so deeply about your country that you take it as your duty to hold it accountable to its highest values and to fight to make it the very best it can be. Under this definition, these athletes and coaches are role models of American patriotism.

As the number of players, coaches, and officials raising their voices in dissent grew, public reaction to those voices was, at best, inconsistent—or, at worst, subject to a racist double standard. The president never let up on his criticism of protesting athletes, even after he left office in 2021. But while he constantly clapped back at James, Curry, Black athletes at every level, and women athletes like Rapinoe, he never responded to the increasingly loaded barbs from Popovich, Kerr, or Van Gundy. It was as if he didn't feel the same power to control the speech and actions of white men as he did others.

This became a running theme during that administration, from Trump, his supporters, and all who rejected the concept of protest overall. They targeted Bubba Wallace, and NASCAR itself, throughout the quest to ban the Confederate flag and to investigate the noose in his garage. Far less rage was directed at the white racers who supported Wallace, verbally or on their march with him on the track.

When Bruce Maxwell brought kneeling to baseball in the fall of 2017, he caught hell from all the usual sources. His white teammate, Mark Canha, who stood by him and placed his hand on his shoulder for support, never caught a fraction of the flack.

This was not isolated to this current era, either. Norman was not the only white athlete in Mexico City who supported Smith and Carlos after they raised their fists on the medals stand. When Jesse Owens was sent by the U.S. Olympic Committee (USOC) and the International Olympic Committee (IOC) to confront the two sprinters and warn the remaining American athletes not to repeat the protests or else risk expulsion as well, he was met by, among others, the members of the national rowing team, a contingent from Harvard, who committed to standing by their Black teammates. Those members—including Paul Hoffman, Andrew Larkin, and Curt Canning—had publicly supported the OPHR, had met with Edwards, and had done behind-the-scenes work in an (ultimately futile) effort to recruit white athletes to the side of the potential protestors.

The rowers, all white, stood with Smith and Carlos, even arguing with Owens, who was shaken badly by the reaction from all the young athletes. Later, the USOC threatened to expel the rowers from the Games as well, but it relented. It also sent a letter to Harvard, claiming that the rowers' stance represented "serious intellectual degeneration" at "this once great university."

Even with white support for Black activism in America, some things have never changed.

7

MEXICO CITY BEFORE, DURING, AND AFTER THE SILENT GESTURE

As the 1968 Olympic Games in Mexico City approached, the only thing that Tommie Smith and John Carlos knew for sure about what they would do in support of the Olympic Project for Human Rights (OPHR) was that they were going to do *something*. No matter who else planned to do anything, no matter what those people might or might not plan to do, and no matter who would be there in person (a crucial consideration—Dr. Harry Edwards would not be at the Games in person, an absence he would attribute to mounting death threats), Smith and Carlos were committed to making some kind of statement.

One way or another, Smith and Carlos were going to be part of a national contingent that was going to leave a mark on a nation that had its grip on the necks of its Black citizens and on the Olympic track and field record books. The expectation was that the U.S. team would be one of the best of all time in the sport and would leave a legacy surpassing that of the team's achievements of 1936 in Berlin, of 1960 in Rome, of 1964 in Tokyo, and all the others. In the end, the men and women track and field competitors won fifteen gold medals, six silver, and seven bronze. (Contrary to popular belief, that includes Smith's gold and Carlos's bronze—neither the U.S. Olympic Committee [USOC] nor the International Olympic Committee [IOC] stripped them of their medals after their protest, and both men have their medals to this day.) The team set four world records, including Smith's winning time in the men's 200-meter final and Bob Beamon's men's long-jump record that broke the previous record by more than two feet and itself lasted for twenty-three years.

What was not clear was how the Black U.S. athletes would act once they had decided not to boycott the Games entirely, as Edwards, Smith, and others had discussed openly in the year leading up to Mexico City. The organized boycott of the New York Athletic Club (NYAC) meet at Madison Square Garden earlier in the year had been something of a test run, and the major athletes and several teams inside and outside the United States had honored it. The national track and field federation had held two sets of Olympic trials—the latter in Lake Tahoe, ostensibly to replicate the high-altitude conditions of Mexico City, but partially in the hopes of warding off a boycott. The potential team members used it as an opportunity to keep discussing what to do until they reached the time to make a decision.

Eventually, after meeting in Lake Tahoe at the trials and then again in Denver before departing for Mexico City, they recognized that too many of the athletes working with the OPHR were going to compete in the Games no matter what. They had various reasons, but many of them centered on the concerns about retaliation by the entities for which they were competing—from the U.S. and the Olympic organizers themselves, from the colleges that they were attending, from the military teams that they were part of while they were enlisted, and many others. The USOC and the infamous Avery Brundage, the president of the IOC and the most powerful presence in the U.S. Olympic movement, had already issued public and private threats about what would happen to any athlete who either boycotted the Games or demonstrated at them. The specter of bans from international competition and the stripping of eligibility for college and national competitions hung in the air throughout the lead-up to Mexico City.

Also, more than ever, the specter of violence from one entity or another was in the atmosphere. Not surprisingly, reports of the New York meet boycott were laden with innuendo that Edwards and the organizers would incite violence in the streets of Manhattan, and parties who didn't want to see athletes finding their voice jumped in to fan those proverbial flames. The athletes, of course, did nothing violent in any way, but the tease of a violent outbreak of angry, uncivilized Black mobs—a tactic always ready to be used by opponents to civil rights—was employed readily and constantly. It was also an explanation hinted at by the organizers of the two sets of Olympic trials—the claim that protestors might take over the meet in Los Angeles justified the need for a second meet in Lake Tahoe.

Real violence, though, put the incendiary rumors of violence in perspective. Martin Luther King Jr. was assassinated in April 1968; a year earlier, King had shown his support for whatever action the Olympic athletes wanted to take by not only saying so in speeches and interviews but by speaking at a large meeting of athletes in Los Angeles in late 1967, a meeting attended by Edwards, Smith, Carlos, and other San José State athletes. In June, Robert F. Kennedy was assassinated as well, in the middle of his campaign for the Democratic presidential nomination. At the party convention later that summer in Chicago, police brutalized young antiwar demonstrators in full view of the network cameras in town to cover the nomination.

Violence was practically assured to greet the athletes from the U.S. and around the world in Mexico City as well. Citizen revolts against the Mexican government's oppressive tactics throughout the year began to increase as the Olympics approached. There already was resentment against the presence of the Games them-

selves, a familiar opposition to money being poured into a spec-
tacle to impress visitors and, in this case, what was expected to be
the largest international television audience for an Olympics to that
point. In a scene that would be repeated too frequently in future
years in other host cities, the poor were displaced, driven away, and
bullied to make way for venues, lodgings, and other amenities. Lo-
cals were at their breaking point. The largest demonstrations, and
the ones most bothersome to government officials, were held by
students at the two largest universities in Mexico City.

As the American athletes debated boycotts and other actions
in the U.S., Mexican students led another march into the Plaza de
las Tres Culturas in the Tlatelolco neighborhood of Mexico City.
The demonstrators were peaceful and, understandably, unarmed.
As they listened to speeches and chanted their approval—among
the topics was further denunciation of the Games' presence—
government soldiers began firing into the crowd. A stampede ensued, and by the time the chaos had ended, as many as four hundred
people, mostly students, had been killed. Reports later emerged
that the shooters were primarily members of a special force gathered specifically for security related to the Olympics. But at the
time, much of the world was convinced that the Mexican government had slaughtered protesting students in a public bloodbath,
less than two weeks before the Games were to begin.

The U.S. athletes who were talking about making some sort of
statement about their oppression in their own country were horrified by the news. It also built their resolve. Carlos and Smith later
spoke of their urge to do something at the Games in honor of the
slain Mexican demonstrators.

Their resolve grew as the track and field competitions commenced. The Black U.S. athletes took over . . . and then declined to
do anything as the medals haul got underway. Smith, Carlos, and
San José State classmate and OPHR partner Lee Evans didn't necessarily believe it would be left up to one or more of them to make
a statement, but as more events ended and opportunities went un-

used, they realized that it *would* be up to one of them. For what it was worth, though, they weren't particularly surprised at that development. The biggest early winner for the U.S. was Jimmie Hines, who set a world record in winning the men's 100-meter dash and broke the ten-second barrier. Hines had made it clear in the run-up to the Games and during the planning meetings that any boycotts and protests would go on without him because he wasn't going to risk his chance at certain stardom—on the track, in endorsements, and even in a likely shot at pro football—by blowing it now. The athletes had bounced around ideas about how to make their feelings known if given the chance, and a few of them revolved around somehow confronting Brundage if he were present for the medals ceremony or were the one hanging the medals around their necks. The options considered included refusing the medals if they came from him, centering a gesture around him, and turning their backs on him. As it turned out, Brundage stayed out of the in-person medals ceremonies. Nevertheless, Hines accepted his gold and stood for the national anthem without disruption of any kind.

Later, Smith would recall in his autobiography:

> Every once in a while I see an interview with him where he blames me for [his] not becoming a superstar after Mexico City. Honestly, I don't have time for that lack of intellect. If he thinks that John Carlos and Tommie Smith messed his career up, then he didn't have one anyway. . . . I wish he'd grow up and stop thinking that I ruined his future.

Hines's view of the protest did illuminate a fundamental split in how the athletes in Mexico City regarded the moment. In the early 1990s, Hines told a reporter that his biggest beef with the protest was that Smith and Carlos never told their teammates what they planned to do, and if they had, he was sure that he and the rest of the squad would have talked them out of it. His belief—echoing the narrative formed by the journeys of Jesse Owens, Joe Louis, and even Jackie Robinson—was that the Black U.S. athletes' dominance at those Games would have had a greater effect on the cause for freedom than the protest would.

"What we did on the track would have sent a strong enough message to all the world and to all races about what blacks could achieve in America," Hines said. "What they did was wrong."

It would be safe to say that the Black athletes who openly oppose Colin Kaepernick, LeBron James, and other athletes who speak out or demonstrate resistance today exhibit the same mindset. The drawback to that, however, is that such an approach gives cover to those who guard the status quo and yearn to keep outspoken Black athletes in their place, reminding them that, yes, the track and court and field and ring are their approved places.

This was the backdrop, then, for the other occurrence at the Mexico City Games revolving around the American flag—George Foreman's winning a boxing gold medal and celebrating by walking around the ring, waving miniature flags clutched in each hand.

Foreman's role in that display, and in the broader context of the Games and the protest, remains complicated. It became obvious soon afterward that Foreman had been put up to the stunt by his coach, Pappy Gault, in a blatant attempt to counter what Smith and Carlos had done. As Carlos points out in his autobiography: "This was held up by the media as a brilliant patriotic response to our 'black-fisted thuggery.' . . . George was the person who loved his country and loved the Olympics: the 'good' black athlete." Foreman was just nineteen at the time and truly did see the Games as his opportunity to shape his life on his own terms after growing up in poverty and crime in Houston, but, as he has said multiple times in the years since, he had no desire to show up Smith and Carlos or the movement. His recollection has always been that he returned home, expecting adulation for his victory, only to discover that everybody in his neighborhood had posters of Smith and Carlos with their fists raised and that he was being called a sellout.

The athletes who threw their support behind those two, how-ever, did so with full force. One of the most noticeable athletes standing up for them was Beamon, after his record long jump. It was enough of a stunning feat to get the world's attention, and, following the lead of Smith and Carlos, he took full advantage of it, taking the podium, accepting his medal, and standing for the na-tional anthem while wearing black socks pulled all the way up and his pants legs rolled up. He threw a fist in the air as he descended the podium afterward. (Ralph Boston, the bronze medalist and the team member who organized and ran the final meeting to discuss boycotting and protesting before the Games, stood on the medals stand barefoot.)

It was Beamon's tribute to Smith and Carlos. Earlier in the year, he had been one of the few Black athletes to cross the picket line and compete in the NYAC meet. His reasoning then was that as a Queens native, he would not get another chance soon to come back to his hometown from where he was attending college, at Texas–El Paso. However, between then and the Mexico City Games, he and eight Black teammates at Texas–El Paso boycotted a meet with Brigham Young University, in protest of the racist theology and practices of the Mormon faith governing the school. Beamon and the others were expelled from the team and had their scholarships pulled, with the Games in Mexico City six months away.

The support for Smith and Carlos on the track continued. The American women, all Black, won gold in the 4 × 100-meter relay. Wyomia Tyus, the latest product of the Tennessee State "Tiger-belles" dynasty that had produced Wilma Rudolph, had also won her second consecutive gold in the 100 meters. In both events, from heats to finals, Tyus had worn black shorts instead of her USA uniform shorts, her choice of protest in the spirit of the pre-Games discussion. When the members of the relay team spoke af-ter their victory, Tyus said that their gold medal was dedicated to Smith and Carlos. Hers was the loudest and most-publicized state-ment on the protests made by a woman throughout the process—a development that, in hindsight, Smith, Carlos, and Edwards have said that they regret, because it revealed how male-centered all the protest talk had been for more than a year, unconsciously but effectively excluding women.

Athletes continued to circle their wagons around Smith and Carlos. The climax came with the visit by Owens, at Brundage's request, to the team to tell them to stay in line and put an end to any prospect of further demonstrations. The group of athletes was almost exclusively Black; the exceptions were the U.S. rowing team and hammer thrower Harold Connolly, Smith's roommate in Mexico City until Smith's expulsion. The athletes across the board were angry that the USOC would use an icon of this magnitude, a hero to all of them on many fronts, as a weapon against them . . . and that Owens, whose snubs over the years by the very nation and government that he was now trying to defend were well documented, would allow himself to be used in this way. In his autobiography, Smith recalls Owens being reduced to tears and asking, "How can you do this? I'm the person who's responsible for you being here now. How can you do this to another Black brother?" Carlos writes in his autobiography that he eventually told him, "Mr. Owens, you know if you had stood up in 1936 a little more, we wouldn't have to in 1968."

With all the drama bouncing from one person and location to another, the track competition continued. Evans was now under the greatest scrutiny, as he had been an originator of the OPHR along with Smith and Edwards, even before Carlos's arrival at San José State. Evans had been in all the meetings, from the ones in Lake Tahoe to the one with Owens. He would be competing in the 400 meters and the 4 × 400 relay. Like his teammates, he positioned himself to make the next large statement by winning gold in both events, setting world records in each and leading a U.S. sweep in the 400. But largely because Smith and Carlos had expressed the sentiments of the project already—and were still embroiled in controversy as they were being sent home from the Games—he limited his protest to the black berets that he and his teammates wore on the medals stand for both ceremonies and the fists that they raised afterward. The perception from then on was that after all the talk over the previous months, Evans "did nothing," which was untrue. Smith, Carlos, and Edwards always defended Evans against such accusations over the ensuing decades, going to great lengths to make sure that his role in everything that led up to Mexico City would not be lost to history.

"I guess that's why I like Lee so much now; he stood up under the pressure," Smith would later write in his autobiography. "I mean stood under it, and though he didn't have a chance to do what John Carlos and Tommie Smith did, he stood behind us with his life."

With all the focus on what the track athletes and the heads of the OPHR would do, the one marquee Black American athlete who did choose to boycott the Games has largely been lost to history. In hindsight, it seems like something important was skipped when it becomes clear that Kareem Abdul-Jabbar never played in the Olympics, let alone won a gold medal. Until the Games were opened up to professional athletes after 1988, an Olympic appearance was standard for the greatest college and amateur players that this country has ever produced. It wasn't a matter of if stars like Abdul-Jabbar would represent the U.S. in the Olympics but when. The 1968 basketball team won the gold as expected, and the names on the roster are as recognizable as on any previous or later winners—Spencer Haywood, for instance, essentially made his reputation in the Games, and Charlie Scott, the first Black player at the University of North Carolina, added a glow to his. But it had been anticipated that Abdul-Jabbar, then Lew Alcindor and heading into the senior season of the most storied career in college basketball history, was a no-brainer for the team, and that with his inclusion, the Olympic domination would never skip a beat.

But Alcindor's social awareness was already well developed. He was the youngest athlete invited to the Jim Brown summit in

Cleveland in 1967 concerning Muhammad Ali's draft decision. Later that year, Alcindor attended the Los Angeles meeting in which King spoke and gave his support to the proposed boycott. Alcindor had all but made up his mind by then. He declined the inevitable invitation to try out for the 1968 team.

Abdul-Jabbar describes his thought process in his 2017 memoir, *Coach Wooden and Me*: "White America seemed ready to do anything necessary to stop the progress of civil rights, and I thought that going to Mexico would seem like I was either fleeing the issue or more interested in my career than in justice. I couldn't shake the feeling that if I did go and we won, I'd be bringing honor to the country that was denying our rights."

Among many others, Smith and Carlos respected him for his choice. In 2018, when the two were honored with a Free Expression Award by the now-defunct Newseum in Washington, Abdul-Jabbar gave their introductory speech.

The perspective of the world put the protests by the Black American athletes into a broader context—not that the racist violence taking place in the country was not enough context in itself, but violent suppression had become the order of the day across the globe. There was the massacre in Mexico City on the eve of the Games, and there was the Prague Spring, the democratic revolution in Soviet-occupied Czechoslovakia that year. The Soviet reaction to the Prague Spring was a summer military invasion of the country.

Consequently, one of the most vocal dissident athletes of the global community at that 1968 Olympics was Věra Čáslavská, the defending all-around gymnastics gold medalist from Czechoslovakia who had had to escape to a remote hideout to avoid potential arrest, barely three months before the Games. When she eventually made it to Mexico City, she went with a mission: to show up the Soviets at every chance she got.

Čáslavská got three chances, winning three gold medals, including a repeat in the all-around. During each ceremony, as the Soviet national anthem played, she bowed her head and turned it to the side, away from the flag. One of her gold medals was shared with a Soviet gymnast—so she turned her head away with her opponent standing right next to her on the podium.

Nobody who was paying attention missed the gesture or forgot it. If it is overlooked today, it's because it was largely unseen, especially in the United States, which was still preoccupied with the rebellious Black athletes. For all the space that the American medals-stand protest takes up around the world, Čáslavská's is just as prominent, or was throughout the remaining years of the Cold War and the Soviet occupation. She was hailed as a hero—"I felt I was lifted off the ground and could perform with ease, defying all gravity," she said in praise of the reception she received for her protest. She was also hailed as a martyr because the Soviet government banned her from competition in the sport for several years.

Eventually when her nation won its freedom, Čáslavská became president of its Olympic committee. She died in 2016, still revered for her own nation's version of the silent gesture.

For many of the fifty years following Mexico City, those involved on all sides of the issue wrestled with its consequences. Those faced by Smith and Carlos are well known, including death threats that continue to this day and concern by both that they still have enemies who would be willing to take their lives every time they appear in public. They feel not fear but awareness: "I've been saved by grace by telling the truth," Smith told the *Sporting News* in 2018. "Truth can set you free; it can also get you killed, and I don't have security anymore. I'm still a target."

Four years after Mexico City, Owens published a memoir whose theme comes through clearly in the title: *I Have Changed*. Smith and Carlos have both said that they reconciled their feelings about the interaction with Owens years later, and both reached out to reconcile with him directly. Carlos said that they ended up conversing; Smith said that he wrote a long letter to him, but he never received a reply and believes that Owens, who died in 1980, might have never seen it. Gina Hemphill-Strachan, Owens's granddaughter, has worked to keep his memory alive and to tie his legacy to those of civil rights leaders who came later, including the ones with whom he clashed most; she appeared on a 2018 panel with Carlos and Edwards at Arizona State University for the fiftieth anniversary of the protests.

Tyus wrote an autobiography in 2018, was part of the protest's anniversary commemorations around the country, and has added her voice to the recollections about 1968 and their relevance to today.

Smith and Carlos themselves have had their personal disagreements with each other, but as the years have passed and their perspective on their protest has grown, they have appeared together more and more often—even more than during the fortieth anniversary of Mexico City, when they received the Arthur Ashe Courage Award at the ESPYS and took part in a return to Mexico City for an ESPN documentary. Again, they shared a panel at the town hall for the fiftieth anniversary at San José State, and both have met and consulted with Kaepernick since he began his campaign for racial justice.

One other surprise reconciliation took place as the big anniversary passed: Smith found himself in close personal and professional proximity, through the then-Oakland Raiders and team owner Mark Davis, with broadcaster Brent Musburger.

In his days as a newspaper columnist, before becoming a noted voice in broadcasting games for the National Football League (NFL), the National Basketball Association (NBA), and college basketball and football, Musburger wrote about the protest at the 1968 Olympics for the *Chicago American*. Among his other condemnations of the two protesting athletes, Musburger writes: "Smith and Carlos looked like a couple of black-skinned storm troopers." Smith and Carlos, and hundreds of others made aware of the remark, scolded Musburger constantly over the decades and demanded apologies or at least recognition of how ugly his choice of words was. Musburger steadfastly refused to even acknowledge the topic.

In the 2021 documentary about Smith by director Glenn Kaino, *With Drawn Arms*, Musburger appears on camera to describe those Olympic Games, his observations, and then to say, at long last, that he had been wrong to write those remarks about Smith and Carlos, and to say that he had apologized to Smith for doing so.

Musburger was eighty-one years old when the film debuted. Smith was seventy-six, and Carlos was seventy-five.

8

MUHAMMAD ALI, THE OPHR, THE BLACK FOURTEEN, AND THE MILWAUKEE BUCKS

Protesting with Your Feet

Playing in the Florida bubbles to conduct or complete their seasons in 2020, with the COVID-19 pandemic still new, was not something that either National Basketball Association (NBA) or Women's National Basketball Association (WNBA) players came to agree on without serious contemplation and, then, important conditions. Even when the leagues agreed to use everything from the uniforms to the floors and the entire arena atmosphere as canvases to communicate social justice awareness, players in both leagues walked away for the season or pushed hard for the entire plan to be scrapped and picked up later, freeing them to commit fully to their causes.

Both leagues and sets of players made it work for a long time, weathering the criticism from outside—and, in some cases, from inside—and keeping their priorities at the forefront. They also played some magnetic, riveting basketball, particularly in the NBA, as it advanced through play-in games and the ensuing first and second rounds. Their plan to make sure that George Floyd, Breonna Taylor, and the Black Lives Matter movement would not be nudged away by the "distraction" of pandemic entertainment was moving along well.

But Jacob Blake was the last straw.

Extreme circumstances demanded an extreme response, and the shooting of Blake by Kenosha, Wisconsin, police officer Rusten Sheskey, on August 23, 2020, even as protest marches and demonstrations in communities all across the country calling for police accountability and reform to use of force dominated the public consciousness, required something extreme. Once again, a bystander had recorded the event on their phone. The video was horrific: As Blake reached for the door of his car, with one of his children in the back seat, Sheskey, standing behind him, fired seven bullets into his back. Blake has been paralyzed since.

The constant stream of recorded inhumanity and indecency inflicted on Black people by the police had passed the point of trauma porn years earlier—at least as far back as 2016, when the murders of Alton Sterling and Philando Castile were played on a loop for days on devices and newscasts around the world. (The breaking point for many others had come more than a year earlier, when North Charleston, South Carolina, officer Michael Slager fatally shot Walter Scott as he ran away from him after a traffic stop. The video also appears to show Slager planting a taser near the mortally wounded Scott; his subsequent police report claims that Scott had grabbed the taser and that officers had tried to revive him, none of which is proven true on the video.) By this point, the raw wound opened by the airing of the infamous Rodney King videotape in 1991 had been torn open further in the era of camera phones, social media, and twenty-four-hour-a-day news cycles.

Blake's shooting, however, came far too soon after Floyd's killing, also caught on camera, to be tolerated by watchful athletes demanding change, especially with Taylor's shooting still completely unresolved, with the Louisville police continuing to protect the officers accused of killing her in her bed. The NBA, the WNBA, and the National Hockey League (NHL) were the major leagues most on everybody's radar at that point, with the NFL still weeks away from its opener and with Major League Baseball's (MLB's) shortened season having only been partially completed.

The Milwaukee Bucks, in the middle of their play-off series against the Orlando Magic, raised the stakes on protest exponentially almost immediately, the most obvious reason being that the shooting took place in their home state. The day after the shooting, and the day after the video went viral, the state national guard was called into Kenosha, charged as usual with quelling violence by protesters who took to the streets demanding accountability. A day after that, Kyle Rittenhouse, a teenage boy with a rifle who had driven to Kenosha from his home in Illinois, walked through the police cordon on the street under the pretense of helping local Kenosha residents protect their property from demonstrators and shot two people to death and injured another.

The Bucks' play-off game against the Magic was scheduled for the next day, August 26. They refused to play. For several hours— days, in some cases, and in other cases from then on—their decision was characterized as a boycott. It was, in fact, a strike: As much as it resembled the refusal to participate in a business's activities that usually defines a boycott, the collective, coordinated, and sudden walkout by the workers here bore the characteristics of a wildcat strike.

Simultaneously, at the WNBA's bubble site, three games were scheduled for August 26. The Washington Mystics, however—the defending league champions as well as the team from which Natasha Cloud had opted out of the season to pursue her social justice causes—refused to play. When they walked onto the court to announce and explain their decision, they wore white T-shirts, which was a noticeable change from the black shirts and warmups that league players had worn as statements four years earlier. White, however, worked better to show off Blake's name spelled out across several players lined up . . . and to show off the seven red bullet holes drawn on the backs of each one.

Ariel Atkins of the Mystics spoke for her teammates—and for the players across the league—in her on-court interview with ESPN that night: "We're not just basketball players, and if you think we are, then don't watch us. You're watching the wrong sport because we're so much more than that. We're going to say what we need to say, and people need to hear that. And if they don't support that, I'm fine with that."

Back in the NBA bubble, Bucks players George Hill and Sterling Brown took turns reading a statement on behalf of their teammates:

The past four months have shed a light on the ongoing racial injustices facing our African American communities. Citizens around the country have used their voices and platforms to speak out against these wrongdoings. Over the last few days in our home state of Wisconsin, we've seen the horrendous video of Jacob Blake being shot in the back seven times by a police officer in Kenosha, and the additional shooting of protestors. Despite the overwhelming plea for change, there has been no action, so our focus today cannot be on basketball.

When we take the court and represent Milwaukee and Wisconsin, we are expected to play at a high level, give maximum effort, and hold each other accountable. We hold ourselves to that standard, and in this moment, we are demanding the same from our lawmakers and law enforcement. We are calling for justice for Jacob Blake and demand the officers be held accountable. For this to occur, it is imperative for the Wisconsin State Legislature to reconvene after months of inaction and take up meaningful measures to address issues of police accountability, brutality, and criminal justice reform. We encourage all citizens to educate themselves, take peaceful and responsible action, and remember to vote on November 3.

Plenty of fans did not support what the players did—and as the rest of the NBA play-off teams, all of the WNBA teams, teams in the NHL and MLB, National Football League (NFL) players in training camp, dozens of college football teams, and tennis players at the Western & Southern Open in New York (an important U.S. Open warmup) eventually canceled or postponed games and other activities, the number of people who railed against athletes again inserting "politics" into sports grew.

Bill Russell, though, supported the Bucks and every other team who walked out.

"In '61 I walked out [of] an exhibition game much like the [NBA] players did yesterday," he posted on social media the next day. "I am one of the few people that knows what it felt like to make such an important decision. I am so proud of these young guys. It reminded me of this." Under his salute, Russell posted a newspaper clip of his quote during his playing days that he would quit basketball "without hesitation" to help in the civil rights movement.

"It would be the duty of any American to fight for a cause he strongly believes in," he is quoted as saying in the clipping.

Russell was referring to the time when he, his Black Boston Celtics teammates, and the Black players on the St. Louis Hawks refused to play an exhibition game in Lexington, Kentucky, in the fall of 1961. It wasn't the first time one of the Black pioneers of the NBA made that choice in the first decade-plus after the league's integration in the 1950–51 season.

In 1959, during Elgin Baylor's much-anticipated and celebrated rookie year with the Minneapolis Lakers, a road trip to Charleston, West Virginia, for a game against the then-Cincinnati Royals began with a blatant slap from Jim Crow: The hotel refused to let Baylor have a room, citing its policy against serving Black guests. Decades later, Baylor told of how he could overhear the desk clerk telling the head coach that Baylor couldn't stay, but when he walked to the desk to hear it for himself, the clerk refused to speak directly to him. To his eternal credit, the Lakers' owner, Robert Short, pulled the team out of the hotel and found another on short notice—a Black-owned hotel, the only one that would admit Baylor. (Short has been vilified, and rightly so, for moving teams away from beloved homes to cash in on new untapped markets: those Lakers, from Minneapolis to Los Angeles, and baseball's Senators, from Washington to Dallas–Fort Worth, where they were renamed the Texas Rangers. But in an NBA that was still wrestling with widespread integration even at the beginning of the 1960s, the owner always received high marks for how he addressed it on the Lakers.)

Baylor was satisfied enough to plan to play that night . . . until he and some Black teammates went to a nearby restaurant and were refused service. It was the last straw, and Baylor refused to play the game. The group of Charleston businessmen who had organized the game and backed it financially, largely because of the draw that Baylor represented, was angry enough to complain to the league office and demand that it punish him. The league refused, and so did the team; they backed Baylor completely. The fans in Minneapolis backed Baylor as well, doubling the attendance when the Lakers returned for their next home game.

Around that same time, during a record-setting college career that led to a legendary pro career, Oscar Robertson traveled with his University of Cincinnati teammates to Houston for a game against North Texas. As Robertson tells it in his 2003 autobiography, *The Big O*, his head coach, George Smith, knocked on his hotel room door around midnight and told him that he had to pack up and move out of the hotel into a room on the campus of historically Black Texas Southern University, because the hotel manager was not going to accommodate a Black guest, even one staying with the visiting team. Robertson recalls seeing quotes from Smith that the thought had crossed his mind to pull the entire team out of the hotel, forfeit the game, and fly back home. Instead, this, from Robertson: "As much as it bothered me that this hotel wouldn't let me stay there, I was just as bothered at being the only person who had to move. All the talk about being a team and winning and losing together, staying together and doing things together—as a team. What just happened?"

At the game the following night, in Denton, Texas, Robertson not only saw a black cat hurled into the locker room; he also was cursed at, called slurs, and had garbage thrown at him during warmups. Again, Smith, his teammates, and the program did nothing about it. After the game, when the team returned to campus, Robertson told Smith that if he ever was separated from the rest of the players again the way he had been in Houston, he would leave the team.

Russell's boycott came a few years later, during the exhibitions preceding the 1961–62 season, when the Celtics' Black players were turned away by restaurants in Marion, Indiana, and Lexington, Kentucky, on consecutive days before games. When it happened in Lexington, Russell, his Black teammates, and the Black players on the Hawks, their opponents that night, refused to play. Russell and his teammates declared that they were going back to Boston, and Red Auerbach ended up driving them to the airport after trying to talk them out of leaving. The game went on with only the white players participating—angry white players, at least from the Celtics, who had spoken out on behalf of their teammates on both nights after the snubs at the restaurants.

Years later, Russell and his surviving teammates would remember the support that the Celtics' players had given them, even when they chose to play without them.

One of the two Hawks players who joined the walkout was Cleo Hill, a rookie from historically Black Winston-Salem State University and the first-round draft pick of the team—led by stars Bob Pettit, Clyde Lovellette, and Cliff Hagan—who had lost to the Celtics in the last two NBA finals (and beaten them for the 1958 title). Unlike the Celtics, who not only had been integrated for the past decade but had built their dynasty around Russell, the Hawks had only integrated three years earlier . . . and the veteran core of the team, by numerous accounts, resented Hill for reasons that showed several signs of being racial.

For the record, Hill and the three stars all denied that race was ever a factor in how Hill's career imploded prematurely. In addition, it has never been established that the resentment throughout training camp and into the regular season had roots in Hill's decision to boycott the exhibition game. The facts say that the coach who drafted Hill and supported his play and development, Paul Seymour, was fired early in the season; the Hawks went on to a losing season; and Hill was released after the season and never played in the NBA again.

It is jarring to grasp that nearly sixty years after his own bold decision, the now eighty-seven-year-old Russell had to witness another group of NBA players taking a similar step, in the realization that, relatively speaking, circumstances had not changed. Materially, Black athletes were then better paid and had better accommodations available to them than the members of their race in overall society. But they were also as vulnerable to the naked racism of that same society as every other Black person—in Russell's case, the Jim Crow laws in the South in the 1960s, and in the Bucks' case, the disproportionate subjection to police brutality. It escaped few people's notice that Brown, one of the Bucks players who read the statement, had been the target of such mistreatment just two years earlier. He had been harassed, shoved, and then tased by Milwaukee police officers while he sat in his car in a handicapped space. Later, one of the eight officers on the scene that night mocked and taunted him with racist remarks in a social media post. That officer was fired. The Milwaukee police department eventually reached a settlement with Brown for $750,000.

Brown was the embodiment of the level to which the players, for all the smirking about how pampered and entitled they were, were not and would never be immune to the treatment that any Black American could be subjected to at any time. Whether one believed in the power of a players' strike or not, that could never be reasonably denied.

One person in the NBA's orbit made it known that he understood where all the Bucks, the rest of the league players, and the WNBA players were coming from. Kenny Smith, the longtime NBA player and longer-time studio co-host for the popular TNT show *Inside the NBA*, took in the sounds and words of the players' walkout, and, while on the air that night, announced that he was walking out with them in solidarity. Smith unclipped his microphone and left the set. That visual had as much staying power as the empty court in the bubble and the sight of players in both leagues standing in unison.

The Bucks and the players across the NBA and the WNBA had a weapon at their disposal that they wielded when they believed that they had no others left. Russell had done the same. So had Baylor nearly three years earlier, after his own case of blatant Jim Crow treatment in Charleston, West Virginia. Those legends were not able to shut their own teams down (the white players in both instances played the games without them), but their point had been made. This time, by the time the dominos had fallen, the entire sports world had shut itself down—barely after it had gotten itself running again after the rapid shutdown from COVID-19 in March. And it did so because Black athletes in the leagues considered to be the Blackest of all deemed that those games had to shut down because if they couldn't be treated like the American citizens and human beings that they were, nobody would get to enjoy the pleasure of being entertained by them anymore. Not until they said so. Not until they got their satisfaction.

A strike was one weapon that the Black athletes gave serious thought to unholstering for the 1968 Olympics. They chose otherwise—and certainly Tommie Smith and John Carlos took an approach that made an indelible impression for all time. But the threat of a boycott will also remain part of the story of those Olympics, of that quest, and of the history of athlete activism forever.

Once again, the DNA for the walkout of 2020 can be found in the lives and actions of the primary figures in 1968.

The dry run of a potential protest, remember, had taken place at the New York Athletic Club (NYAC) meet earlier in 1968. It was the biggest statement the Olympic Project for Human Rights (OPHR) had made to that point. The NYAC had made itself a convenient target for activism, with its decades of restrictive memberships that barred Black people and Jewish people—an observation that the club constantly denied. But the agenda for the OPHR, of course, was much larger.

Two of the demands that the OPHR listed were to reinstate Muhammad Ali as the world heavyweight champion and to continue to ban the apartheid regimes of South Africa and Rhodesia from the Olympics. Flexing the boycott muscle on behalf of those demands, in turn, showcased the power of the tactic even more.

South Africa and Rhodesia were banned from the Olympics because of the pressure from African nations—some of them freed from colonial rule just within that decade—who threatened to boycott every competition in which they were allowed. The International Olympic Committee (IOC) tried to slip both nations back into eligibility for the 1968 Olympic Games; the unified Black African nations and the OPHR's pressure pushed it to reverse this decision and keep them out again.

As for withholding services to force substantial change . . . Ali fit snugly into that category. His refusal to step forward to enlist in the U.S. Army during the Vietnam War after he had been drafted has rarely, if ever, been referred to as a "boycott." His justification for refusal was as a conscientious objector and as a minister of his still relatively new Muslim faith. His opponents, of course, labeled him a draft dodger—five decades later, after his death in 2016, there were still scattered references from those who hated him for this stance. A few even purposely called him by his dead name, the one that he left behind upon his religious conversion: Cassius Clay. More than forty years after the last holdouts among mainstream news outlets stopped calling him "Clay," or "Clay, aka Muhammad Ali," those who were insulted by how he stood fast in his beliefs stayed insulted beyond his natural life.

In 1968, though, he was still Clay, the exiled champ. It took two more years for his license to fight to be reinstated, and three more before his draft evasion conviction was overturned by the Supreme Court. (As a sign of the current times and of the power of a very old narrative, when Donald Trump in 2018 finally pardoned Jack Johnson for his egregious and indefensible conviction in 1913, the president also offered to "pardon" Ali. The idea was never mentioned again, possibly because he was reminded that Ali's legal slate was clean and had been for decades.)

The Black athletes formulating their plan for the 1968 Olympics had the nation's attention. The NYAC meet, one of the first major events at the relocated and renovated Madison Square Garden, was the best opportunity to find out who was really listening. Dr. Harry Edwards and the OPHR found out quickly that, in essence, everybody was.

Tommie Smith, John Carlos, and Lee Evans, for starters, immediately declared that they wouldn't run, wiping out top competitors in no fewer than six marquee sprint events. The names began to fall as athletes of all races, from all colleges and clubs, and from around the world, weighed whether it was in their best interests to defy the boycott, show their faces, endanger their relations with each other and with the sport—or, in a worst-case scenario, face possible disturbances and arrests inside and outside the Garden.

The Soviet Union backed out. So did Villanova University, a track hotbed, and most of its fellow Eastern institutions. Athletes either declared their support for the boycott or conveniently found reasons to skip the event. That included two members of the celebrated University of Southern California (USC) 4 × 100-meter relay team: Earl McCullouch and O. J. Simpson, the favorite for that year's Heisman Trophy. Larry Livers, one of the nation's top high hurdlers, planned to attend and, according to an account in *Sports Illustrated*, was headed into the Garden but was stopped by a pair of boycotting athletes and, on the spot, talked out of competing. Ken Noel, another classmate of Smith and Carlos, confidant of Edwards, and a member of the OPHR, stood in front of one team bus and blocked its path into the Garden; eventually, the driver backed out and took another route into the arena.

Most accounts show that only nine Black athletes ended up competing. One of those athletes was Bob Beamon, who deliberated and then decided that the chance to go to his hometown from his school and team in Texas was worth it. (Beamon had an awakening of his own later in the school year, and by the time of the Olympic Games, he was an adamant supporter of Smith and Carlos.)

Another was Lennox Miller, a sprinter from USC, native of Jamaica, and future Olympic champion (and father of Olympic gold medalist Inger Miller), who was quoted in *Sports Illustrated*: "I am not in favor of discrimination by the New York AC, but I don't want to be dictated to by outsiders."

Many who had wanted the Black athletes to just keep their mouths shut, be grateful, and perform on cue denounced the boycott as it was happening. None could label it a failure, though. It kept the IOC and U.S. Olympic Committee (USOC) on alert in the months leading up to the Games. It also convinced the IOC to rescind its order allowing South Africa and Rhodesia back into the 1968 Games, just two months after reinstating them. Finally, it left enough of a bruise on the NYAC that later in the year, it canceled the 1969 meet. It still took years before a notable number of Black people and Jewish people were accepted as members of the club, and it did not begin allowing women to join until 1989, after fighting it in court throughout.

In a way, the dry run of a boycott at Madison Square Garden had a dry run of its own. The year-plus leading up to Mexico City was a busy one. In the fall of 1967, before the meet boycott in New York, and before the meeting in Los Angeles attended by the OPHR organizers and by Alcindor, Smith and Edwards organized a demonstration against the unfair housing practices that they and their fellow Black athletes and other Black students endured in and around their own San José State campus. They planned a peaceful demonstration for the season-opening home football game against Texas–El Paso— and, as a bonus, announced that if the housing situation wasn't corrected immediately, the Black players would not play in the game.

School president Robert Clark, fearing a confrontation at the stadium but also recognizing the seriousness of the situation because of the threatened player walkout, agreed to start opening housing for Black students all over the city. But he also canceled the game out of fears for fan and student safety, thanks to the usual vague threats of violence from angry Black demonstrators. No less than the then-governor of California, Ronald Reagan, lashed out at the decision to meet protestors' wishes, demanded that Clark resign as president, and accused him of exercising a "policy of appeasement."

The following year, after the Mexico City Olympics, San José State's Black football players again waved the boycott flag, this time in protest of their opponent, Brigham Young University (BYU), and the Mormon Church's then-openly discriminatory doctrine against Black clergy. The San José State student council supported the boycott and demanded that the game be canceled. The game was played, but the Black players made good on their threat and refused to participate.

The spirit of direct engagement was growing in college sports, and Black athletes were losing every inhibition against making their voices heard. The 1969 season saw the most notorious example of not only Black college football players flexing their muscle on behalf of civil rights but the white establishment in higher education and throughout sports harshly retaliating. That season, fourteen Black players at the University of Wyoming—undefeated and ranked twelfth in the national polls at the time—went to head coach Lloyd Eaton to tell him that they wanted to wear black armbands in their upcoming game against, again, Brigham Young. Black students on campus were planning a demonstration against the Mormon Church's discriminatory policy against Black clergy; the players were equally angry about racist treatment from players and fans during a road game at BYU the year before.

None of that mattered to Eaton, who immediately kicked all fourteen players off the team and, according to the players, showered them with slurs and epithets and scolded them for breaking his rule against political activism. He later was quoted as saying that the players "slapped the state of Wyoming in its face." The school and most of the students stood behind the coach; the white players on the team were torn. The season quickly went downhill, with the team losing its last four games of the season. The fourteen Black players were never readmitted to the team; it took nearly fifty years before the players and the school even began trying to reconcile the rift.

The Black Fourteen incident has been the reference point for every protest by Black college athletes since—including the 2015 Missouri football team's pledge to boycott the upcoming season in support of Black students' fight against the school's administration over their treatment by professors, fellow students, and the president and chancellor. That president and chancellor resigned soon after the football team took its stance.

In 1970, a year after the conflict at Wyoming, nine Black Syracuse football players (for still-unexplained reasons labeled "the Syracuse Eight") boycotted the spring game after the university and athletic officials ignored months' worth of demands for equitable treatment with white students in school and on the team. The players were immediately suspended from the team—and they countered by refusing to play regardless of whether the coaches and administration reinstated them, eventually sitting out the entire season. Again, it wasn't until the mid-2000s that the school reached out to heal the wounds with the players.

The norm at the time was that boycotts like this brought change at a painfully slow pace. The cities where Baylor, Russell, and other NBA players refused to play took their time in changing their laws about lodging and dining accommodations. The football players at Wyoming and Syracuse saw almost nothing happen for a long period after they took their stands. The regular activism against the Mormon Church and Brigham Young took several more years to pay dividends. The NYAC remained stubborn in its membership practices for years, remaining a practically all-white amateur club as everything in the amateur sports and Olympics universe changed around them.

The IOC's quick reversal on South Africa is one of the exceptions; so was San José State's reaction to the first football boycott threat in the dispute over equal housing rights. To the school's credit, Clark, the president, not only heard the complaints and acted on them, defying the governor along the way, but also was one of the biggest names to go against the grain and praise Smith and Carlos for their medals-stand protest in Mexico City. The closing words of his statement of support were cherished by Smith, Carlos, and everybody involved: "I hope that their gesture will be interpreted properly. They do not return home in disgrace, but as the honorable young men they are, dedicated to the cause of justice for the Black people in our society." For that sentiment, Clark was bombarded with hate mail that approached the volume that Smith, Carlos, Evans, and Edwards received.

More recently, the Missouri football team got a response that showed that the university understood the power of those athletes as more than a vehicle to generate millions of dollars in revenues. Of course, it can never be assumed that massive cash loss isn't the main motivator for entities to take action when athletes wield their leverage this way. Even when those institutions consider losing games or losing fans, the money that goes with them is always a factor.

There are few better examples of the influence of money on the pace of change than the 1965 boycott by Black players at the American Football League (AFL) postseason All-Star game, scheduled for New Orleans. When one by one they were subjected to the city's Jim Crow policies as the game approached—cabs refusing to pick them up, restaurants refusing to serve them or even admit them, hotels not honoring their reservations, and one bar owner threatening them with a gun—they met, got the support of many of their white teammates, and began flying out of town, intending not to come back for the game.

Players would later say that they did not do this to try to force change in the city or in the league—they simply wanted to be treated with the respect that they were entitled to and could not care less whether the game was played. But as soon as news got out that Black players were catching flights home, the AFL bosses met, did some quick renegotiating, and moved the game to Houston. It shook the business community in New Orleans to its core—the city was pushing hard to get a pro football team, either in the AFL or in the NFL, and this loss would deal a crushing blow to their hopes. It was a dilemma facing several southern cities at the time, as the discrimination entrenched in their laws threatened to block expansion or relocation of football, baseball, and basketball teams. Atlanta wrestled with it while trying to get an MLB and an NFL team.

Major alterations in city laws and policies soon followed, and the Saints began play in the NFL in 1967. Had Jim Crow remained unchecked—and had the Black players had not called the city on it—the league might have gone elsewhere.

The NBA players' collective stoppage of play on behalf of Blake had purpose and results envisioned as well. As the Bucks' players were planning to strike the play-off game, they were also trying to contact Wisconsin attorney general Josh Kaul and lieutenant governor Mandela Barnes, explaining what they were doing and demanding to know what the state executives planned to do. Kaul and Barnes, in turn, pressed the state legislature to take up the police reform bills that were going nowhere at the time.

"The Bucks have, frankly, done more to address these issues than [members of the legislature] have done," Kaul later told reporters. "I applaud them for stepping up and playing a leadership role in the debate."

In New York, Japanese-born tennis star Naomi Osaka, whose father is Haitian, explained why she stopped playing in the wake of Blake's shooting. "Before I am an athlete, I am a black woman. And as a black woman I feel as though there are much more important matters at hand that need immediate attention, rather than watching me play tennis," she wrote in a social media post. "I don't expect anything drastic to happen with me not playing, but if I can get a conversation started in a majority-white sport, I consider that a step in the right direction."

Osaka raised the volume on the conversation at the 2020 U.S. Open, an event she had won in 2018. With the tournament policies requiring masks while not in action due to the pandemic, Osaka put the name of a different fatality from law enforcement brutality on each mask that she wore to a match. She conducted most of her postmatch interviews with the mask on and the name showing. She wore seven masks for the seven wins needed to earn the title. The last one read "Tamir Rice," the twelve-year-old boy shot to death in 2014 by police in Cleveland while sitting in a park, a toy gun tucked into his pants. Officer Timothy Loehmann was never charged in the killing. (Every name she wore represented someone who had died; Blake survived.)

Osaka would win that tournament. During the on-court interview during the trophy ceremony, Osaka was asked what message she had hoped to send with the names on the masks. Her answer: "What was the message that you got, is more the question."

All the aforementioned sports paused for a few days following the police shooting of Blake and debated among themselves about the appropriate time to return. NBA and WNBA players put conditions on their return. One of them was even more of a commitment by the two leagues to dedicate their arenas and facilities to serving as voter sites. It was what Cloud and others had emphasized regularly throughout the summer's rise of social awareness. The teams had moved toward that goal in fits and starts. Suddenly, with the weight of players staying away—and, in the NBA's case, putting a hold on the play-offs—teams sped up the talks with their cities, states, and elected officials, and the voting centers opened, with several cities equipping two full arenas for voters. That, remember, included Washington, D.C., where Cloud had demanded that the

Mystics' building be used to make sure that the most-overlooked citizens had access.

The walkout by the basketball players lasted three days, landing this exhibition of athlete power under the category of fast results. With so much not really having changed at all over the decades, seeing that change following direct action was welcome.

9

HOW O. J., MICHAEL, AND TIGER
DROPPED THE BATON

"Passing the baton" is such an appropriate metaphor for handing the responsibility for leading the fight for freedom and equality to the next generation. You don't have to have ever run track—and the athlete asked to pass the baton doesn't have to have ever run track—to grasp the image. Even when it seems as if there is no actual finish line, whatever is out there at the end to mark victory gets closer with every handoff.

This particular race has not been a straight line—no line that connects Jack Johnson to Jackie Robinson to Bill Russell to Tommie Smith and John Carlos to Mahmoud Abdul-Rauf to LeBron James to Colin Kaepernick to Naomi Osaka can ever be described as "straight." But one way or another, the relay continues, and the hopes that someone is out there to take the baton next remains alive.

But the baton has been dropped a bunch of times. Or the next runner never showed up on the track. So often, it was the superstar, the world-record holder, the odds-on favorite, the one who could have won the race and ended the competition by himself who blew the exchange.

The Michael Jordans. The O. J. Simpsons. The Tiger Woods-es. The list is excruciatingly long. But those names are at the top. They're the place to start.

"They would've been the handoff," Kenneth Shropshire, the Global Sports Institute leader and sports and society scholar, told the *Sporting News*. "But they didn't [take it]."

Every library in America could be filled with the theories on the obligations of celebrities to use the platform they have to change the world for the better—not just how they could but whether they should. But, as Paul Robeson famously said, it is always a choice. Throughout the history of this country and society, athletes of the greatest status and magnitude have chosen not to try, not to sacrifice what they have, not to put the effort that they put into building and ascending that platform into using it as a means to wrench society in the right direction. They have chosen to let someone else take the next handoff, to drop the baton and leave it where it lands, to skip the race altogether.

When asked, or told, or ordered to shut up and dribble, they dribbled.

Those choices broke the continuum. They created a chasm, spanning a good four decades, in the history of athletic resistance that always has to be explained away. That chasm has inadvertently inflated the activists of the 1960s in stature, even beyond the impressive truth of their own accomplishments, and shed a different light on the pioneers who preceded them. It demands study of how the movement found a way to restart after it hit that dead spot and of how the activists of today use the decisions of the greatest names in the annals of sports as cautionary tales, faults to avoid or to overcome.

This absence of activism among the great ones of this period invites a reevaluation of the standards of greatness itself. As activism has continued to expand throughout the 2010s and early 2020s, the legacy of James and his place in National Basketball Association (NBA) history has been debated constantly, endlessly (and largely annoyingly, thanks to the stubborn inability to frame the eras of play to fairly analyze each one's stars). The argument has frequently gone off on wild tangents. But one tangent that on the surface seems the most illogical actually offers a fascinating window into what the basketball-admiring public deems the most important.

In other words: yes, debate the numbers all you want, the championships, the trips to the finals, the marketing, the global draw, the visceral impact on the game, the approach to the finances. But off the court, as a role model, as an advocate for his people, as someone constantly willing to speak out and act out against the systems that need to hear and see it—to use the platform to its fullest? Who could rationally argue that James doesn't beat Jordan hands-down?

That has been the cloud over Jordan throughout his public life, or at least since he started the journey to become the figure that he is, as a professional with the Chicago Bulls in the mid-1980s. That cloud didn't come into truly sharp focus until 1990, when he made the notorious comment on political engagement that would cling to him from that moment on: "Republicans buy sneakers too."

To make a long story that's been recited for more than three decades short: In the 1990 race for the U.S. Senate in North Carolina, a Black Democratic candidate, Harvey Gantt, was facing the incumbent white Republican, Jesse Helms, one of the most repellant figures in the long, loathsome history of Southern political racist demagoguery. Public pressure began to mount for Jordan, who had grown up in Wilmington and was an icon under Dean Smith at North Carolina, to endorse Gantt and call for an end to the tyranny of Helms's tenure once and for all. Jordan did not, and Helms won by a narrow margin. While it seems to many that they had been hearing the reported Jordan quote since at least the middle of that race, the quote about sneakers would not actually be seen in print until 1995, in a Jordan biography by Chicago sportswriter Sam Smith, *Second Coming*, tied to Jordan's return from his basketball retirement and his detour into pro baseball. But the silence that the quote excuses was enough.

Jordan spent years dancing around whether he ever actually said those words. Even if he largely was not believed, fighting his plausible deniability was ineffective. He may or may not have been misquoted, and it may or may not have been blown out of proportion, but it was such convenient shorthand for his choice of riches over activism that it was certain to live forever.

Then came the spring of 2020, and he stopped dancing . . . in *The Last Dance.*

The ESPN documentary series about his career and the end of the Bulls' 1990s dynasty was filmed, produced, and edited with Jordan's approval, so there was instant skepticism about how transparent he would be on the most controversial moments of his career. How he addresses the "sneakers" comment gives one answer: He admits that he said it and tells why.

It was "in jest" and "off the cuff" with his teammates, Jordan says. He actually supported Gantt that year but did not want to publicly endorse somebody he did not know. He never thought of himself as "an activist" or "a politician," but as someone who poured all his energy into basketball and did not regret it.

Everything revealed in *The Last Dance* about the heartless, remorseless competitor that Jordan was confirms all of this self-characterization. But nothing illustrates his stance on speaking out more than this statement:

It's never going to be enough for everybody, and I know that. I realize that. Because everybody has a preconceived idea for what I should do and what I shouldn't do. The way I go about my life is I set examples. If it inspires you? Great, I will continue to do that. If it doesn't? Then maybe I'm not the person you should be following.

It fairly screams out, "That's not my baton. Keep that away from me. I've got my own race to run."

To understand Jordan, though—and to understand those who largely walked in his footsteps, single-mindedly toward their safest careers and not toward speaking out—it is best to go backward. It seems cruel to tie him to Simpson, in light of what Simpson's public image has become and what is revealed about him in yet another ESPN-produced documentary series . . . but Simpson was the next best candidate for the continuum, and he strode right past it.

Simpson, remember, was a titanic figure in American sports even while in college, long before the National Football League (NFL), TV commercials, movies, broadcasting, live courtroom drama, and the tabloid life. He was big enough to cast a shadow over football and track and field—which places him back in the chaos of the run-up to the 1968 Olympics. With the Games taking place in the unusually late time frame of October, he chose not to compete for a berth on the U.S. team in favor of playing his senior year of football at the University of Southern California (USC). He was going to continue his sprinting mastery that spring, until Dr. Harry Edwards and the Olympic Project for Human Rights (OPHR) staged the boycott of the indoor meet at Madison Square Garden. Simpson found an excuse not to attend, splitting the difference between honoring the boycott and not sounding like he was giving in to a group of Black agitators who scared much of the white sports hierarchy.

He was far from alone in making that choice—Jimmie Hines, the eventual Olympic 100-meter champ and lifelong resenter of Smith and Carlos, backed out of the meet as well, hinting that his life had been threatened. (Edwards, in fact, has been quoted as suggesting that Hines needed to remember his football prospects and stay healthy for them by honoring the boycott, but whether that was intended to be a threat is up for interpretation.)

In the documentary on Simpson, *O. J.: Made in America*, Edwards recalls talking to the soon-to-be Heisman Trophy winner about using his name, talent, and visibility for the movement that Edwards was heading up. He was personally aware that Smith, Carlos, and Evans were just as big and had as much to lose as Simpson did, but they were always vocal, present, and willing to face real danger on behalf of the cause. That didn't move Simpson, Edwards says, providing arguably the definitive quote of the series about its subject.

Edwards says that Simpson's explanation for staying clear of all of that was "I'm not Black, I'm O. J."

It was not only an ethos by which Simpson lived (until a certain high-profile trial years later); it was one that U.S. advertisers bought into and sold to its sports-loving audience. When he hit major stardom in the early 1970s, by breaking the two-thousand-yard single-season rushing mark and becoming one of the faces of the NFL back when doing so in Buffalo seemed impossible, he put himself in line to become one of the very first widely marketed Black athlete endorsers. This was still new territory—one that was punctured and finally blown apart in a big way by Nike and the aforementioned Jordan. Hank Aaron, while chasing down and breaking Babe Ruth's home-run record, was still a scarce sight on commercials. Such basketball icons as Julius Erving were still a few years away from prominent ad time. The famous Mean Joe Greene Coca-Cola commercial, in which he throws his jersey to a little boy at the game, hadn't been made yet. Simpson cleared the way with his Hertz ad campaign, which began in 1975 and is still a legend in the industry, with images of him racing through airports and leaping over suitcases, accompanied by the earworm of a jingle: "the superstar in rent-a-car."

Through the documentary, though, viewers see how carefully these images are curated. No other Black face is shown in the spots. The elderly woman who cheers him on ("Go, O. J., go!") is designated to be white. The commercial and its central figure are designed for maximum inoffensiveness. Simpson went along with it and reaped the rewards.

That exemplified the 1970s, the decade following the one that had ended with war in Southeast Asia still raging, antiwar demonstrations, assassinations seemingly coordinated to put a halt to the civil rights movement, and an Olympics protest that split the nation and sports. Sports in the 1970s seemed purposely constructed to reverse course on the activism of the 1960s. The 1980s and, in some ways, the 1990s appeared to strive to keep the momentum going. These decades put the 1960s in the rearview mirror, with athletes straying further from what the Alis, Russells, and Smiths and Carloses stood for and not fearing the negative comparisons.

Thus the observations about dropping the baton, and of that period being a wasteland for athlete activism, the opposite of the principled 1960s. Compare, for instance, the reactions by two prominent athletes to whom Edwards reached out at volatile times. Simpson said what he said. Edwards also made a point to connect with Toni Smith-Thompson after she made her protests during the national anthem as a senior off the beaten path at a Division III basketball program.

"The costs have been different for me," Smith-Thompson would later tell the *Sporting News*:

> Because I wasn't a professional, I wasn't on an Olympic stage, it didn't strip me of a career because I didn't have one, or my endorsements because I didn't have them. But it's a real loss. . . . It's not just losing an activity, it's really losing a part of my identity. The court is often where I drew my achievement, my abilities, my excellence—the court was always the place where I could exercise mastery.

As extraordinary as her sacrifice was, in that context it was even more so. Simpson chose not to sacrifice anything.

Woods, the standard-bearer of the 1990s and 2000s, ascended the stage just as Jordan and his final act with the Bulls was exiting. Woods, though, resolutely aligned himself with Jordan on the rigid wall separating himself from outspokenness on any subject besides his sport—and, eventually, by embracing Donald Trump.

A case could be made that Woods flung the baton away most egregiously of all. The argument rests on the promise that came not only from his ascent in golf, the ultimate country-club sport, one that had steadfastly kept Black people in their place at the expense and service of white people, but also in the tease of breaking those doors down forever.

Woods's father, Earl, became famous himself for his vision of the effect that his son would have on the world, through his dominance of his sport and the sports landscape as a whole. His actual words have been mangled over the years: Earl did not actually tell a reporter that Tiger would have a greater impact than Nelson Mandela, Gandhi, and Buddha, but he was asked whether his prediction covered the impact that those figures had had. His answer, however (in the *Sports Illustrated* cover story when the magazine selected Tiger as its 1996 Sportsman of the Year), is still grandiose:

> He has a larger forum than any of them. Because he's playing a sport that's international. Because he's qualified through his ethnicity to accomplish miracles. He's the bridge between the East and the West. There is no limit because he has the guidance. I don't know yet exactly what form this will take. But he is the Chosen One. He'll have the power to impact nations. Not people. Nations. The world is just getting a taste of his power.

Nike built its initial marketing campaign around that theme— "I am Tiger Woods." It was prophecy, in a way: The demographics in the galleries changed overnight. So did the demographics of those playing the game at nearly every level. Players on the tour today, male and female, claim him as an influence growing up. Earl's logic about his son's potential global reach was sound. But in hindsight, the athlete who fit those parameters best, in his prime and afterward, was Muhammad Ali. Tiger, however, only gave the most superficial acknowledgment of the racial barrier-breaking that he represented. Like Jordan, he made his game the limit of his influence, preferring to be an example. He refused to speak out on anything, when his voice—and, as his father said, his larger forum— could have changed everything. Nike's inclusive, expansive slogan ended up occupying a similar space as Simpson's ethos of "I'm not Black, I'm O. J."

The greatest star of his era, a Black man yet again, shied away from any obligation to use that influence. The world more or less accepted it—and, of course, portions of the world applauded it, in the unshakeable belief that athletes, especially Black athletes, should conduct themselves exactly that way.

By 2016—when Kaepernick began kneeling and when Trump was elected president—the bar of expectations for Woods was essentially on the floor. It couldn't sink much lower once the world was reminded that, like Tom Brady and many others, Woods and Trump had moved in the same celebrity circles for a long time. The two had known each other throughout Woods's public life. They had golfed together often and continued to do so during Trump's term. When the president's online campaign against protesting athletes started to rage endlessly in 2017, Woods had no discernible reaction. After a tournament in Paramus, New Jersey, in August 2018, a reporter asked him what it meant, or should have meant, to be friends with someone so openly contemptuous of Black athletes in particular. Woods said, "Well, he's the president of the United States. You have to respect the office. No matter who is in the office, you may like, dislike personality or the politics, but we all must respect the office."

The office, in turn, honored Woods. Shortly after Woods won the 2019 Masters after a long, injury-induced drought, Trump awarded him the Presidential Medal of Freedom. The honor had historically recognized a high standard of contribution to American society and culture by civilians, and Woods certainly fit the criteria, no matter which chief executive would have someday rewarded him. But at that point, this president was handing the medals out like rewards for patronage and loyalty, signified by the fact that he also gave one to shamelessly racist and misogynist radio host Rush Limbaugh. The Woods award gave off the stench of a gift to an old pal, a boast about all the famous people whom Trump knew, and a middle finger to everyone who castigated him for his constant condescension and smears directed at Black athletes who weren't properly humble and grateful.

That baton had hit the ground long before. The promise of Earl Woods years ago now comes off as a mean-spirited joke, in the same category as the once-innocent-sounding racial and ethnic designation that his son had created for himself: Cablinasian. (In one of his first major TV appearances after his breakthrough Masters victory in 1997, the then-twenty-one-year-old Woods told Oprah Winfrey that the term described his Caucasian, Black, American Indian, and Asian heritage. His multitude of Black fans recoiled at what appeared to be a minimization of his Black identity.)

Compare Earl's grand notion of where Tiger could go with the skill and opportunity he had to what Dr. Glenn Bracey, a Villanova sociology professor, said (in a 2018 *Sporting News* interview) about those opportunities in the proper hands:

> That's why black athletes are such potentially powerful activists. It's not just that they have platforms, it's not just their visibility, it's not just their money. It's that their physical being is a public display of competence, of discipline, of overpowering whites quite often, that is a permanent opportunity to display opposition to white supremacy.

The athletes who approach the position that Woods held—and potentially still does—are not the stars of the sports with large Black participation and followings. Serena and Venus Williams, Osaka, and, from earlier eras, Arthur Ashe and Althea Gibson fit more neatly into Woods's category. Tennis holds its own with golf as a white-dominated, white power–supporting, elitist, and separatist sport. All of those players affirmed their allegiance to the cause. Ashe may have done so more courageously than the others (at the risk of minimizing the oppression that the Williams sisters and Gibson have endured as women as well); when the rest of the activist sports world demanded separation from South Africa and its apartheid allies, Ashe fought to get into the country, speak his truth to power, and reach out to the Black majority to give them access to his services and his play. Collectively, they did not shirk their duties—they didn't even seem to consider them duties.

Woods was, and is, fine with letting others carry that load.

While the 1970s, 1980s, and 1990s came off as the era of disconnect, the current era that encompasses Kaepernick's protests tends to reveal disconnects as well. If indeed everyone with a platform faces a choice, then the choices that many have made reveal much about who they are and who they very likely would have been in previous eras, whether around Johnson and Robinson and Robeson and the 1968 Olympics . . . or in the desert that followed.

Jerry Rice, for instance, stands alone as the unquestioned greatest wide receiver who ever played the game, and as one of the two or three greatest football players of all time. His origin story has become legend, from his upbringing in Mississippi, helping his father build houses, catching and throwing bricks and building his legendary hands in the process, and then emerging from historically Black Mississippi Valley State University and setting numerous college receiving records—and still being passed over until the sixteenth overall pick in the 1985 draft, before embarking on an unprecedented twenty-year run of excellence in the NFL.

Even as someone who didn't share with the world his personal beliefs on society, or possibly *because* he didn't share them, Rice remained a benignly beloved figure long past retirement. Then Kaepernick began kneeling . . . and Rice's reaction online was this: "All lives matter. So much going on in this world today. Can we all just get along! Colin, I respect your stance but don't disrespect the flag."

Rice was immediately dragged all over social media, to the point where plenty of online posters (not just anonymous trolls, but recognizable NFL followers) decided tongue-in-cheek to demote Rice on their lists of all-time greatest receivers, from first to roughly three thousandth. Rice had to apologize a day later, claiming that he had been unaware of the Black Lives Matter movement. It was not convincing in any way. It was even less convincing four years later, when Rice and several former 49ers teammates attended a White House ceremony at which Trump issued a pardon to the team's former owner, Eddie DeBartolo Jr.—who had been suspended by the NFL and forced to give up control of the team in 1997 after a bribery conviction. It was one of many pardons handed out by that administration to cronies who had been convicted of or had pleaded guilty to crimes.

All the former players in attendance heaped praise on the former owner; Rice made sure to add, "I take my hat off to Donald Trump for what he did." By that time, in early 2020, Trump had also spent considerable time slandering NFL players and all athletes who protested, without a word of reaction from Rice.

As for the jibes about where he now stood on the list of all-time greats in the hearts of fans . . . in 2018, Randy Moss was inducted into the Pro Football Hall of Fame, and as he gave his acceptance speech, he wore a tie on which the names of thirteen victims of police violence were embroidered. (Moss may have started a trend that bears watching in the near future: A year later, safety Ed Reed eschewed the standard polo shirt under his Hall of Fame jacket as he was introduced at the Hall of Fame exhibition game, instead wearing a T-shirt with the faces of nine victims of police violence.)

Rice was far from the only active or former NFL player who, facing the renewed scrutiny of how they chose to use their platform ushered in by the Kaepernick era, chose to either sidestep any mention of the rise in activism by their brethren or to push back against it, and against Kaepernick specifically.

Black fans had regularly come to Michael Vick's defense after the explosive, genre-shifting quarterback's return to the NFL after serving time in federal prison for his notorious dog-fighting conviction. By 2017, he had wrapped up his thirteen-year playing career when he went on a football studio show on the Fox Sports Network to talk about what might be next for Kaepernick, who had not been signed in the season following his protests.

"The first thing we got to get Colin to do is cut his hair," Vick said. "I don't think he should represent himself in that way in terms of the hairstyle. Just go clean-cut. Why not?"

He went on to explain that he was thinking about the image and perception that Kaepernick projected and that trimming his lengthy Afro "ha[d] to be a start for him."

Almost everything Vick has said since then about Kaepernick, and about advocacy in general, has been tainted by that comment. Like others who expressed that Kaepernick had to "do something" to get back in the good graces of the league and its supporters, Vick was trashed mercilessly for pandering to exactly those people. Seeing an iconic figure like Vick fall prey to stereotypes about "dangerous" looks or "unacceptable" hairstyles, and the respectability politics that accompany them, was hurtful to many. Vick soon backtracked, insisting that what he said "was not in malice," but also not taking back his words.

Vick's soundbite disappeared from the public's radar soon after. The 2018 observations of Dak Prescott did not wash away as easily. They may have been from currency bias, borne of Prescott's being an active NFL player, unlike Vick, Rice, and others who would not engage or who missed the point when they tried to. But a factor in how Prescott addressed the climate in the league and in society at the time was clearly who he was, what position he played, and what team and owner he played for.

Quarterback is exactly the influential position it's portrayed to be. "Quarterback of the Dallas Cowboys" raises the influence, power, and visibility a few more notches. Owner Jerry Jones, meanwhile, had not only scolded his players about kneeling or otherwise protesting during and after the time Kaepernick had sparked the movement; he had put his weight behind the NFL's punishments against kneeling during the anthem that were so oppressive that the league and players' union soon agreed to halt putting them in effect. On top of that, Jones clearly had a line of communication to the White House, curried the president's favor, served as his conduit to other owners . . . and even was mentioned as a party in Kaepernick's labor grievance over his blackballing.

That is the context in which Prescott—who had risen meteorically from fourth-round pick to starter and focal point on the league's marquee team and a play-off contender—spoke about anthems, flags, kneeling, and other activism. Jones had just declared that he expected his players to stand respectfully for the anthem, with "toe on the line." Prescott—born and raised in, again, Mississippi—was asked during an interview session at the Cowboys' training camp what he thought about using the anthem as the backdrop for protest:

> I don't think that's the time or the venue to do so. The game of football has always brought me such a peace and I think it does the same for a lot of other people, people playing the game, people watching the game, and any people that have an impact on the game. So when you bring such a controversy to the stadium, to the field, to the game, it takes away. It takes away from the joy and the love that football brings a lot of people.

The reaction by many was summarized in a six-foot-by-ten-foot mural spray-painted by local artist Trey Wilder on a wall in West Dallas the next day: the face of Prescott, in pads and jersey, as the main character in the horror-racism movie *Get Out*—a character who is hypnotized into falling into "the sunken place," a space of obedience and appeasement to the movie's white community. The imagery was spot-on, and those who felt let down by Prescott's bending to Jones's authority found it hilarious.

Prescott did not literally "get out" of Dallas; three years later, in early 2021, he signed a massive contract extension to stay with the Cowboys for the near future. Cowboys fans debated whether he truly was the quarterback to return them to glory. Over time, his acquiescence to the owner faded as a topic.

Cam Newton never got the *Get Out* mural treatment. He did, however, create the standard for distancing oneself from the protest movement that Prescott had challenged. Plenty of eyes turned to Newton in 2016, when Kaepernick's protests first came to light. One of the early theories about the long-term success of Kaepernick's efforts was whether fellow players would support him, and which players would—that is, would the league stars stand up for him, protest themselves, or even support his position? Newton became a major focus because he was in as unique a position as any player ever has been—one of the only Black quarterbacks ever drafted first overall, the league's reigning Most Valuable Player (MVP), a man who had led his Panthers to the Super Bowl the year before, and someone who had worn his individuality on his sleeve throughout his career, including that previous year, when he was constantly scolded by fans about his on-field celebrations and his postgame fashion choices. Their verdict: That man, regardless of whether he was one of the most magnetic and dangerous players in any given game, needed to be more humble.

Newton addressed the elephant in the room in a press conference at the Panthers' headquarters as the Super Bowl approached in early 2016, when he said of the relentless criticism: "I'm an African-American quarterback that may scare a lot of people because they haven't seen nothing they can compare me to."

Much of the nation's Black fandom appreciated his bluntness. They were less appreciative the following season when, after a protracted stretch of silence on the burgeoning protest issue, Newton expressed his feelings during an interview with ESPN. To summarize, he had found the fence, and he was going to straddle it as best he could:

> What I can't, you know, fathom is, how does one-eighth of an inch—something so small—be the difference and such a big commodity in our whole lifetime. And that's the thickness

of our skin, one-eighth of an inch. Under that, we're all the same color, and that's the big picture.

On Kaepernick, a colleague and someone he respects as a competitor—once, when the teams met, they switched off doing each other's signature touchdown celebrations—Newton said: "Who am I to say that it's wrong? Who am I to say that it's right? Either or, it's still personal."

The lines seemed fairly clearly drawn on who would embrace the spirit of the 1960s and give the 2010s and 2020s a chance to be compared favorably . . . and who was more aligned with the void between those eras. Naturally, the lines weren't as distinct as one would assume. Into the fray, again, came Jordan. In July 2016— after the killings of Alton Sterling and Philando Castile and after the ESPYS speech by the NBA stars, but before Kaepernick began protesting—Jordan took to the pages of ESPN's *The Undefeated* to do very much what he had insisted he would never do: Get involved.

"I am saddened and frustrated by the divisive rhetoric and racial tensions that seem to be getting worse as of late," Jordan writes. "I know this country is better than that, and I can no longer stay silent. We need to find solutions that ensure people of color receive fair and equal treatment AND that police officers—who put their lives on the line every day to protect us all—are respected and supported."

With that, he announced $1 million contributions to two organizations: the National Association for the Advancement of Colored People (NAACP) Legal Defense Fund and the Institute for Community-Police Relations, created by the International Association of Chiefs of Police.

A few looked askance at a massive donation to a police organization in that climate—but even with that, it was not just incredibly generous, it was publicly so, as Jordan had become someone who steered far from publicizing his charitable efforts, even ones that belied his reputation as someone who didn't reach out to help his own people. More importantly, it was his most definitive public statement on behalf of freedom, justice, and equality of his life.

It was a quarter century after "Republicans buy sneakers too."

Yet as proof that no one who wades into those waters can wade back out easily, in 2018, Jordan was pulled into the then-latest stage of Trump and James's war of words. In an interview with CNN, James answered a question about what he would say to Trump if he were sitting across from him by stating, "I would never sit across from him." The president weighed in on social media with a reply that was, as often was the case, not new to the tactics of white supremacy—use one prominent Black man as a weapon against another. "I like Mike!" he posted.

Jordan was not a personal friend of Trump, however, as his fellow 1990s icon Woods was. He also was no longer focusing his energy on playing at the expense of speaking up.

"I support LeBron James. He's doing an amazing job for his community," Jordan replied.

Time will tell whether the long-overdue baton handoff went cleanly.

10

STICK TO SPORTS AND ENJOY
YOUR WHITE HOUSE TRIP

Michael Jordan's playing days were not without occasional rebellious moments. Craig Hodges claims he witnessed one. When Hodges and his Bulls teammates visited the White House after their 1991 National Basketball Association (NBA) championship—the visit to which Hodges brought the letter he wrote to President George H. W. Bush—Jordan was not at the ceremony. According to Hodges's book, Jordan said in the locker room the night when the Bulls clinched the title, "I'm not going to the White House. Fuck Bush. I didn't vote for him."

Over the span of four decades and five administrations, starting with Jimmy Carter's term, champions and championship teams have made the White House trip a destination. The presidents made it so that the invitation was understood, that the champs were to expect them, that it would become one of the perks of ultimate victory. Each president, or their libraries or families or whoever and whatever safeguards their cherished memories, has a treasure trove of team jerseys with their names on them—Reagan, Bush, Clinton, Bush again, Obama. The photo galleries of grinning presidents and grinning players and coaches is enormous. It's part of Americana, so much so that it still comes as a surprise to many that it's only a very recent addition to Americana. There are engravings of Andrew Johnson and black-and-white photos of Calvin Coolidge hosting sports teams, but what we know of the tradition is all in vivid color video. (According to the White House Historical Association, two baseball teams in 1865 were the first sports teams to visit the White House, and Coolidge was the first president to host a championship team when the 1924 Washington Senators baseball team visited.)

Skipping the visit for any reason was a rare exception, so rare that for years, most people could name those who'd skipped off the tops of their heads. Often, individuals just had better things to do, excusing their way out of it. Even more rarely, the athletes stayed away in objection to the president, his policies or words, or party. Two of these jump to mind from Barack Obama's time in office: Tim Thomas, after the Boston Bruins won the 2011 Stanley Cup, and Matt Birk, after the Baltimore Ravens won the 2013 Super Bowl.

One other snub stands out more in hindsight than it did at the time: After the New England Patriots held off the Seattle Seahawks at the goal line to win the Super Bowl in 2015, Tom Brady blew off the White House trip, chalking it up to a scheduling conflict. It felt like nothing more than the team megastar big-timing the leader of the free world, following in the footsteps of Jordan and others. It was practically part of the tradition, not having 100 percent attendance and not having one or two of the biggest names on hand.

In a relatively short amount of time, the White House visit became a staple of championship celebrations, alongside parades, banner raisings, the Stanley Cup being used in not-family-friendly ways, and fans setting bonfires in the streets.

Then came the 2016 elections.

The day after Election Day, and just before the Cleveland Cavaliers were greeted by President Obama at the White House in honor of winning the NBA championship, Richard Jefferson posted on social media: "Words cannot express the honor I feel being the last team to visit the White House tomorrow."

The day after the trip, LeBron James was asked whether he would visit the White House and its newly elected occupant if his team won another championship. "I don't know," he replied. "That's something I would cross . . . we'll have to cross that road, I guess. We'll see. I would love to have to cross that road."

Soon after that, in an interview with *Complex* magazine, the Cavaliers' Iman Shumpert was asked the same thing. "I'm not going to the White House," he said.

All of those refusals could have been chalked up as "just" a group of basketball players, Black ones at that, and at least one (James) who had publicly endorsed the president's opponent, Hillary Clinton. It could also have easily been chalked up to virulent animosity toward the president-elect, by a representative group of people, but not something that would lead to other teams in that sport or any other to take the same course of action. This was well outside the norm. This remained so, even in the midst of a National Football League (NFL) season dominated by the continued protests by Colin Kaepernick. (At this point, Kaepernick was the 49ers' starting quarterback, and on his team and across the league, players were supporting him by kneeling, sitting, raising a fist, linking arms, or putting hands on or around shoulders.)

The champion Cavaliers had lit a spark, though. It was time for players and teams to address it. The Patriots and the Atlanta Falcons realized that when they arrived in Houston for Super Bowl LI the last week of January 2017. Barely a week after his inauguration, President Trump instituted the notorious Muslim travel ban. One of the very first tangible outgrowths of the ban was fans and media from across the country and around the world traveling to Houston for the game and running into mass protests at airports, along with lawyers setting up in and around the terminals to render aid to travelers going back and forth from countries affected by the ban.

At the annual Super Bowl media day, the players, coaches, and staff on each team congregated in a room for an hour to entertain questions (and to have entertainers question them). They were asked several times what they thought of the president's order, about the president period—and whether they would visit the White House if they won.

Between then and the week following the Patriots' overtime comeback win over the Falcons to claim another Lombardi Trophy, four players announced that they were not going to go, including Chris Long, who had put a needed white face on the support of Kaepernick; Devin McCourty, one of the first players outside the 49ers to protest, by raising his fist; and Martellus Bennett, the brother of the Seahawks' Michael. Dont'a Hightower also skipped it, but he had brushed off the trip two years earlier as well, and he had made the trip after Alabama's national title.

This was now a trend worth watching—a platform that had always been available, and one with the potential of having more power than all the others. This was unprecedented access that could only be earned one way. (In that way, it fit seamlessly into the concept, embraced by Tommie Smith and John Carlos, that no real protest could be pulled off if they did not finish first, second, or third in the race.) It had reached a point where the ceremonies were carried live, by some outlet somewhere, so a live audience was likely. If nothing else, it was a ready-made photo opportunity, a moment that could be used for the ultimate publicity—the way that Hodges had used it, to be seen and heard. And, of course, it was access to the holder of the highest office in the land. Using the moment to speak up or to stay away would each send a message that would be hard to ignore.

It also is effective to throw a spotlight on the players—the teammates of those mentioned, for example—who declined to take a side, a stand, a position of any kind except for basking in the glow of the building and its occupant. Those who, in so many words, only wanted to stick to sports. Which was part of Hodges's plan: While he was there, in a dashiki that stood out in contrast to the suits and ties that surrounded him and bearing a letter to the president demanding help for Black people . . . Jordan was not there at all. And the rest of the Bulls were just taking in the sights and reveling in the pomp and circumstance.

Boycotts are potent weapons and effective use of the kind of leverage that celebrities have that the masses whom they're representing do not. If there had been any fear or hesitation for others to use their positions in this way, at the White House, in posing, jersey-brandishing, pass-catching, basket-shooting displays that both sides of the political spectrum have tended to enjoy—that fear was disappearing. The presence of a unifying enemy was helping erase it. And it was happening within a month of the new president's election, and just six months after Kaepernick and his protests had changed the game.

The Patriots, of all teams, wound up being the first team to bring that dynamic to the new administration. As it turned out, Brady did not attend, either—by that time, his bond with Trump had been made public, and it had cast his absence from the previous White House visit with Obama—a persistent target of outrageous criticism on social media by then-private citizen Trump—in a new light. This time, as in previous no-shows, Brady cited family obligations. Head coach Bill Belichick and owner Robert Kraft were present . . . both of whom Trump had thanked, along with Brady, for their support in a speech the day before the election.

But some two dozen players stayed away, when in past visits no more than a handful had skipped.

White House Visit Watch was officially on. So was, as it turned out, White House Invitation Watch.

In 2017, when the Golden State Warriors were in the position that James and the Cleveland Cavaliers had been in the year before—as defending champs debating making the unpleasant visit—Stephen Curry set the storm in motion by saying that he did not want to go. Trump made his memorable dis-invitation, and the players and coach Steve Kerr laughed their way through their even more memorable mocking of the dis-invitation. Most memorable of all, of course, was James's social media retort, the one that started with "U bum!"

Five months later, the Patriots faced the prospect of answering the wave of White House visit questions by reaching another Super Bowl, played in Minneapolis. That city, remember, became a platform for protests against police brutality following Philando Castile's killing just a few miles away from the downtown stadium some two years earlier. The reasons for players to object to making the trip had only increased since the previous Super Bowl, and since the Warriors had dis-invited themselves. Finally, the Patriots' opponents were the Philadelphia Eagles, a locker room full of players unafraid of speaking out—Malcolm Jenkins and Torrey Smith, who had protested during games and were core members of the Players Coalition that had sprang in part from those protests, plus Long, signed as a free agent and bonding with Jenkins and offering himself up as a spokesperson for the growing movement.

The Eagles pulled off the victory, and the questions came immediately. It quickly became the Trump-vs.-athletes battlefield of the day. Definitive plans for a White House visit weren't firmed up until May 2018, setting an early June date, during the Eagles' off-season camp, when the players would be together to make the trip south. As that date approached, the convenience of the players being gathered in one place became increasingly moot. Individuals said outright that they would not go, and the team began discussing whether to go at all.

To that point, the Eagles' Super Bowl win had been a bell-clanging display of the bonds between the teammates and between the players and the city that planned to never stop celebrating the championship that it had been waiting for throughout the entire Super Bowl era and beyond (the last Eagles championship had been in 1960, the first year when the rival American Football League [AFL] played at all and six years before the first Super Bowl). Philadelphia was as split down racial lines as it had ever been, but, in this instance, that residential segregation didn't mean that the city or the region had any significant Trump strongholds—so, besides hugging the Eagles every chance it got, in the barely undercontrol victory celebration and at the victory parade, the people lined up behind the players on the White House visit topic: If the players didn't want to go, the fans were going to be perfectly fine with it.

Trump's response was a rerun of his previous ones: He cancelled the Eagles' visit the day before it was scheduled and trashed the players while doing it. On the day of the celebration, two surreal scenes unfolded at opposite ends of Interstate 95. In Philadelphia, the Eagles players practiced and then stood in their locker room and walked the throng of reporters through their reasoning, their reaction to the cancellation, their process in reaching their decision, and their commitment to each other even on social and political issues that they didn't each see eye-to-eye on. Long patiently explained his point to waves and waves of cameras and microphones—adding, "I have three years of quotes about Donald Trump. I don't feel I should keep going down that road."

Center Jason Kelce, the raucously unquestioned star of the victory parade, said that the communication and respect among the players were an example that the whole country could emulate. And Jenkins did not speak, per se—letting a series of messages written on cardboard speak for him. Many carried detailed information about the causes that he prioritized, on criminal justice and police abuse and immunity. The one that caught the most attention read, "You Aren't Listening."

Down the road in Washington, Trump decided to "honor" the Eagles anyway with a celebration, with invited guests whom he claimed were Eagles fans among the White House's inner circle. The identities of the "fans" seemed questionable, appearing more like props or paid actors, or both, a notion that the players and the actual Eagles fans back home mocked. Trump also had the national anthem performed before the "ceremony" began. An attendee who was never publicly identified took a knee during the rendition and then disappeared into the crowd.

The players and teams who objected to the shenanigans in Washington were beginning to lean hard into the idea of showing up the president by being no-shows for the traditional visit. The event increasingly became a tradition that they could live without.

Before the Eagles made their choices, one other 2017 champion team made a trip to the White House, minus two key players who politely excused themselves. Both Carlos Correa and Carlos Beltrán were very circumspect in explaining why they were not joining their Houston Astros World Series champion teammates. They respected the office of the presidency and understood the disagreements that people had, they both said, but they had other plans. Both are also natives of Puerto Rico, and they were spending enormous time and resources helping their birthplace recover from Hurricane Maria—a task, they made sure to point out, that Trump did not perform nearly enough.

"It was not politics or anything," Correa told reporters. "It was just that the day off was perfect to be able to provide some help for the people in Puerto Rico in need."

Members of the next few World Series champion teams were less subtle. In 2019, after the Washington Nationals won the title, reliever Sean Doolittle—who engaged with the city and its residents and uplifted their causes as much as any active player in the sport—told the *Washington Post* that while he regretted missing the moment with his teammates, "I just can't do it."

Again, a specific atrocity steered him to his decision—early the previous year, Trump had been caught in a meeting putting a heinous label on poverty-stricken Black African and Caribbean nations. "There's a lot of things, policies that I disagree with, but at the end of the day, it has more to do with the divisive rhetoric and the enabling of conspiracy theories and widening the divide in this country. My wife and I stand for inclusion and acceptance, and we've done work with refugees, people that come from, you know, the 's—hole countries,'" Doolittle told the *Post*. He and his wife, Eireann Dolan, not only stay busy with charities and philanthropy but are outspoken about their beliefs and always keep a running conversation on nonbaseball topics on their social media accounts.

So, Doolittle abstained. A handful of others—primarily Series MVP Stephen Strasburg and largely introverted star third baseman Anthony Rendon—skipped it as well. It was soon revealed that the two were long-time friends and golf partners of Trump. It also turned out during the White House visit that several players were enamored of the president and his attention, to the point that they laughed uproariously as Trump jokingly reached around Kurt Suzuki's chest during the catcher's turn at the microphone. Doolittle would have been significantly out of place.

In between the Astros and the Nationals were the 2018 champions, the Boston Red Sox.

The divisions within the team began forming as soon as the talk of a potential White House trip began. The most definitive statement ended up coming from the manager, Alex Cora—like Correa and Beltran, a native of Puerto Rico. "I've used my voice on many occasions so that Puerto Ricans are not forgotten, and my absence is no different," the *New York Times* reported Cora as saying on the eve of the scheduled visit. "As such, at this moment, I don't feel comfortable celebrating in the White House."

Several players also purposely stayed away. All of them were Black American or Afro-Latino; they included Mookie Betts, the reigning American League MVP, and stalwart pitcher David Price. None of the boycotters were white; only a handful of the players who attended were not white. The contrast was impossible to ignore.

By this point, the president's term was not even close to its two-year mark, but the template was in place. The go-or-not-go choice was a vote for or against the man in the Oval Office. It was already certain that whoever won the next election would be measured by this standard—Trump, for whether he would force a reckoning from players and teams about their beliefs, and a possible backlash by Trump supporters among the athletes against a possible successor, as revenge for the snubs of the previous term.

As Trump's term went on, though, the champions continued to debate how to handle the spoils of victory. The Washington Capitals won the 2018 Stanley Cup, with a sizable assist from one of the few Black players who dot the league's rosters, forward Devante Smith-Pelly, who became a home-crowd favorite and rewarded fans with several clutch postseason goals. But as the Cup-clinching victory drew near in the finals—and the odds increased that Smith-Pelly would soon become one of a still relatively few Black players with their names engraved on the venerable trophy—he announced that he planned to skip a White House visit. "The things that [Trump] spews are straight-up racist and sexist," he said, going straight to the point.

He was joined in his intentional protest by two teammates, Brett Connolly and Braden Holtby—the latter of whom was not only the Cup-winning goalie but also outspoken in his support of mistreated communities, particularly the lesbian, gay, bisexual, and transgender (LGBT) community. "You're asked to choose what side you're on," Holtby said, "and I think it's pretty clear what side I'm on."

The trend became more sensitive in the summer of 2019, when the debate traveled from pro and college team celebrations to victories by the national teams in international competitions. On deck at that time was the U.S. national women's soccer team at the Women's World Cup. The U.S. dominates the sport in Cup play and had advanced out of group play, on its way to another victory. The face of the team, again, was Megan Rapinoe. She clearly had shown that she was not afraid to protest, as the first prominent athlete to repeat Kaepernick's kneeling three years earlier. She had decided not to defy the national federation's anti-kneeling rule that had grown from her protests, but during the tournament, she was admonished for not standing obviously at attention and not singing the words of the national anthem aloud. Trump, for his part, had proven time and time again how contemptuous he was of outspoken women, and of outspoken athletes, and he had taken the opportunity to scold her on social media every time she came up in the news. A clash was inevitable; the only way it likely would have been avoided was if the Americans lost.

While the tournament was still going on, Rapinoe told a national soccer magazine, "I'm not going to the fucking White House. No. I'm not going to the White House. We're not going to be invited. I doubt it."

Trump, again, took the bait, answering on social media with a slew of demeaning and insulting comments about athletes in general, Rapinoe specifically, and their ingratitude for the wonderful gifts that America and he himself had bestowed upon them. The president of the United States also said of a team wearing the national colors and representing its highest ideals and performing with great success and dignity—usually a no-brainer for administrative support—"I am a big fan of the American Team, and Women's Soccer, but Megan should WIN first before she TALKS! Finish the job!" Rapinoe, of course, was not talking about winning or not winning; she was talking about having to face the person who was so chronically offensive to her and others.

The players' response was to stand behind Rapinoe on her White House declaration. Rapinoe's response was to strike her iconic, arms-spread pose after a goal in the next game, acknowledging that it was her answer to Trump's incessant needling. They eventually took the title. The team kept its word and refused to visit. The issue became moot when the president never extended a formal invitation, eventually saying after the title-game victory, "We'll look at that."

Invitations to the White House during the Trump administration for women champions generally were never a guarantee. No Women's National Basketball Association (WNBA) champion was invited during his time in office. That should not come as any kind of surprise in light of their unyielding, unapologetic activism from before Trump ever took office. He at least spared the league and its players the kind of targeted wrath that he turned onto Rapinoe. Nevertheless, the Sparks, the Lynx, the Storm (twice), and the Mystics appear to have never even been under consideration for a White House trip. A stretch of activism that began with a protest against police killing Black people and ended with protests against police paralyzing Black people was never likely to include an invitation.

The South Carolina women's basketball team won the National Collegiate Athletic Association (NCAA) championship in April 2017; by September, no hint that they would be invited had come. Eventually, a mass celebration that would include numerous college champions, team and individual, was scheduled for November. South Carolina coach Dawn Staley, a Hall of Famer and a giant in the sport, said that her team would not go. A big part of it was, simply, never hearing about anything for months. "That in itself speaks volumes," Staley said. A year later, the 2018 NCAA women's champion, Notre Dame, also was not invited.

Yet when Baylor won the women's national title in April 2019, Trump set up a team visit before the end of that month. Head coach Kim Mulkey thanked him profusely for inviting them. The Oval Office was packed with Republican dignitaries from Baylor's home state of Texas, which the president lauded for its support of him. It stood out in glaring contrast to every other interaction he had had, or not had, with women's sports champions.

None of the men's basketball champions in 2017, 2018, and 2019—North Carolina, Villanova, and Virginia—were invited to the White House. All three programs and their head coaches—Roy Williams, Jay Wright, and Tony Bennett—indicated that they had no plans to go.

As time went on, every championship celebration left open the possibility of some kind of bizarre or outrageous development.

None seemed as bizarre or outrageous as the visit by Clemson's football team, the 2018 college play-off champion, in early 2019, like Baylor's, taking place mere weeks after their victory.

Twin functions were served by this particular visit. Clemson's head coach, Dabo Swinney, had long ago proven himself to be among the least progressive (or most regressive) and most intransigent voices in all of sports on the topics of racial justice and equality and on the notion of athletes protesting. (His feelings about the rights of college athletes to do anything except play and stay loyal to the university were also far from progressive.) Early in the Trump administration, when the groundswell around the refused invitations by the Patriots, the Cavaliers, and the Warriors was building, Swinney immediately said that he and the school would accept an invitation, and Clemson did celebrate its title that year at the White House. When they won again in 2019, he quickly accepted the invitation again.

The other function served: The federal government was in a partial shutdown, instigated by the president in an attempt to set money aside for his Mexico border wall plan. For the Clemson visit, then, he came up with the idea of catering with fast food: McDonald's, Burger King, and Wendy's. Supposedly, it drove home the point that the government was being run on a shoestring because of the hard-headedness of those who opposed Trump's offensive wall, and the solution was to buy burgers, fries, and nuggets with his own money to show the college kids a good time in the people's house. Never mind, of course, that meals had historically never really been part of a team White House visit—although it did feed a brief controversy over why President Obama had never thought of giving the youngsters a decent meal as Trump had. The punchline, though, was that it was far from a decent meal, yet Trump used it as a photo op—a spread of paper wrappers and burger boxes and dipping sauce in front of a smiling president. Onlookers accustomed to the familiar routines from decades of past White House celebrations recoiled at the sight of the fast food fest and the reason behind it. But the president liked it so much that three months later, he served the national champion Baylor women's basketball team the same cuisine.

The last year of the Trump administration was filled with sports delays and cancellations because of the COVID-19 pandemic. There were no NCAA men's or women's basketball championships awarded. The Los Angeles Dodgers won the World Series after an abbreviated season, with a biracial Black-Japanese manager and with a pair of former White House boycotters in Betts and Price (who each opted out of the season but did receive a championship ring). The Lakers, led by James, won the NBA championship that was delayed by the pandemic pause until October, the month before the 2020 election. Alabama's national college football championship and Tampa Bay's Super Bowl win (led by, again, Brady) came right before and right after successor Joe Biden was inaugurated, respectively. The window closed quietly on the era of flexing the White House boycott muscle.

Relatively speaking, that is. Before the football championships were decided, Trump's campaign to overthrow the election that unseated him in favor of Biden culminated in the violent coup attempt at the Capitol Building on January 6, 2021. How many athletes who supported Trump, believe that the election was stolen from him, and view Biden as an illegitimate president might manifest their beliefs by mimicking the boycotters of the Trump years? This remains to be seen.

The Lakers did not end up visiting the White House in the season following their 2020 championship . . . for safety reasons during the COVID-19 pandemic. The 2020 World Series champion Dodgers, however, were honored by President Biden at the White House in July 2021, and three weeks later, so were the Buccaneers. Brady attended and spoke at the ceremony, his first postchampionship appearance since 2005, when George W. Bush was in office.

Thus, James's 2016 Cavaliers did not end up being the last to visit the White House, despite his teammates' earlier predictions on the eve of the Trump administration. But everything that followed that declaration forever reshaped the neutral, nonpartisan tradition of posing with the president and holding up a jersey. And every individual who excuses themselves from the ceremony will be eyed far differently than the Jordans ever were before.

11

8 MINUTES 46 SECONDS*

Black athletes leaped to post their reactions to the police killing of George Floyd in Minneapolis on May 25, 2020. LeBron James was one of many, and he chose to make the natural and obvious connection. On his Instagram account, he posted a screenshot of officer Derek Chauvin kneeling on Floyd's neck in the street, appearing to stare into the phone recording him. Next to it was a familiar photo of Colin Kaepernick in uniform kneeling on the 49ers' sideline. Above the two photos: "This . . . . . . Is Why." After four years of likely billions of characterizations of police atrocities positioned against the condemnation of Kaepernick for silently protesting in the presence of the flag and the anthem, built around the phrasing "This is why they kneel," James's shorthand was easy to decipher.

It was only the latest example of James taking up the mantle of protest against racism, oppression, and injustice as an active player. Eight full years had passed since James and his teammate and close friend Dwyane Wade had encouraged their fellow Miami Heat players to gather in a hotel ballroom, don hoodies, take a photo, and post it in honor of Trayvon Martin, the Florida teenage victim not only of a fatal shooting by rogue vigilante George Zimmerman but also of the criminal justice system that did not even charge Zimmerman until public pressure became too great. James and Wade explained the choice by saying that they felt obligated to take notice of the crime because they were both fathers and because Martin had been on his way home with the infamous iced tea and Skittles to watch NBA All-Star Weekend. The first serious wave of "keep politics out of sports" admonitions of James's career began immediately.

That, again, was eight years and two teams ago. Between that photo with the hoodies and the end of 2020, James had won three more National Basketball Association (NBA) championships, had weighed in on countless more killings of Black people by law enforcement, and had faced very public challenges to the very right that he had to express himself on anything other than whether his legacy had pulled even with Michael Jordan's.

It didn't take long for each man's devotion to social change and uplift to become part of the criteria that many would use for determining which athlete was the "Greatest of All Time." Could you really be "the GOAT" if you stay on the sidelines when the fight for human rights rages on the field? Or should that ever enter the conversation alongside rings and finals trips?

Regardless, James strapped up and waded into the fight. He was one of the players in the NBA who wore "I Can't Breathe" warm-up T-shirts after several New York City police officers converged to choke Eric Garner to death on camera in 2014. He joined his fellow players in demanding that the NBA sanction Clippers owner Donald Sterling, with the not-very-subtle threat of a league-wide players' strike, after Sterling's volley of recorded racist remarks came to light.

He weighed in during the nightmarish week in July 2016 when Alton Sterling and Philando Castile were killed by police on video and when the Dallas officers were shot to death during a Black

Lives Matter march. That was when he joined Wade, Carmelo Anthony, and Chris Paul on stage at the ESPYS and gave what was, in hindsight, a landmark plea for recognition of the traumas that Black people were enduring—and which still managed to be almost buried in the volcanic events of the next five years.

When James's turn to speak came, he delivered: "Tonight we're honoring Muhammad Ali, the GOAT. But to do his legacy any justice, let's use this moment as a call to action to all professional athletes to educate ourselves, explore these issues, speak up, use our influence and renounce all violence, and, most importantly, go back to our communities, invest our time, our resources, help rebuild them, help strengthen them, help change them. We all have to do better."

James did his part, including starting a public elementary school in his hometown of Akron, Ohio, the I Promise School. (Years later, the students would win the informal competition for cutest presentation ever at a championship-ring ceremony, for their recorded presentation of James's 2020 Lakers ring at the start of the 2020–21 season.) That effort in itself became a target of his antagonists, who, upon its opening in 2018, flung accusations about the school's legitimacy and his commitment to it. Many of those same antagonists had challenged James's honesty and credibility a year earlier, when a racial slur was spray-painted on his home—in short, they accused him of making it up for sympathy and attention.

James's ongoing sparring with Donald Trump commenced during that stretch as well, including the "U bum!" tweet in defense of fellow NBA star and champion Stephen Curry and his refusal, like James, to make the traditional White House visit with Trump in office.

This head-butting with the president also incited the incident that crystallized James's commitment to advocacy, the outraged reaction it instigated, and the unique phrasing of the trope about Black athletes staying in their place and keeping their mouths shut. The phrase became indelibly identifiable with James, and he wisely co-opted it to use in a documentary series shedding light on that very topic. The phrase: "Shut up and dribble."

That was what Fox News prime-time talk-show host Laura Ingraham notoriously told James to do on the night that she went into a tirade about his not having permission or the intellectual capacity to critique the president. What inspired that rant was an interview for a web series, *Uninterrupted*, produced by James's company in advance of the 2018 All-Star Game, conducted by ESPN anchor Cari Champion as she rode in a car with passengers James and Kevin Durant. Among the perspectives the two stars gave on their own lives and the impact their experiences had on informing their current decisions and responsibilities, James identified one of the greatest obstacles they face:

> The no. 1 job in America, the appointed person, is someone who doesn't understand the people and really don't give a fuck about the people.

Ingraham's subsequent on-air command to James to "shut up and dribble" was far from original. Plenty of athletes previously targeted by those admonishments have responded by resuming their activities that were not limited to merely sticking to sports. What James did, though, expanded on that greatly by turning that very phrase against his critics, starting with a social media post of the phrase "I Am More Than an Athlete" and the hashtag "We Will Not Shut Up and Dribble." That was followed by the creation of the three-part documentary series for Showtime that aired later in 2018, titled *Shut Up and Dribble*, about the history and legacy of NBA players who had wielded their influence and popularity to move society forward and push the door to freedom and equality open a few notches more. It gave Bill Russell, Oscar Robertson, Kareem Abdul-Jabbar, and others often overlooked for their pioneering actions their proper due.

A product of James's SpringHill Company, the docuseries was not originally titled *Shut Up and Dribble*. The phrase flung at James to discredit him and shame him into silence ended up being a gift from the publicity gods. Said SpringHill president Jamal Henderson in a 2018 interview with the *Sporting News*, "Timing-wise, it caught fire."

Now, with the nation's temperature spiking as the video of Chauvin's gruesome execution of Floyd ran on a loop everywhere that video could be shown, James kept his feet firmly planted on his platform. He did not keep his activism separate from that platform either, leading the charge among NBA players to bring protest onto the basketball court: in their demands for the bubble, their decisions to kneel together (mostly) during the pregame national anthems, their robust debates regarding whether to opt out of the postpandemic return to play in deference to those who wanted to engage full-time in the movement, their postseason strike on behalf of Jacob Blake, and their attachment of demands to and concessions from the league in exchange for players returning to the court.

That was where the NBA players stood. It was where the Women's National Basketball Association (WNBA) players stood as well, as did individuals in other sports.

The rest of the sports world started drawing up plans on the fly. Those sports' history of activity—and recent lack thereof—came into play, and much of it was nothing that they could be proud of.

The timestamp of "8 minutes 46 seconds" will likely stay attached to the Floyd killing forever. The very first report from the official prosecutors' criminal complaint filing charges against Chauvin on May 29, 2020, four days after the killing, stated that Chauvin had stayed kneeling on Floyd's neck for 8 minutes 46 seconds. The time was challenged soon afterward; within a week, a handful of different times were reported. When Chauvin's murder trial began the following year, prosecutors introduced a different time, one even more disturbing than the original: 9 minutes 29 seconds. It still didn't dislodge "8 minutes 46 seconds" from the public consciousness.

Protests pegged to that time stamp began soon after that first report. Demonstrators in several cities across the country and the world lay down in streets, plazas, campus squares, and in front of buildings for 8 minutes 46 seconds. Television networks went off the air for 8 minutes 46 seconds. Companies—including the ones that were only working remotely because of the pandemic—observed 8 minutes 46 seconds of silence. In the rotunda of the Capitol Building in Washington, Democratic Congress members, with Speaker of the House Nancy Pelosi of California in the forefront, got onto one knee for 8 minutes 46 seconds. Most of them, including Pelosi, wore kente cloth, their symbol of solidarity with the Black victims of brutality and oppression, a choice that came off as more performative than necessary, even for a moment of such gravity.

At times, police officers joined the 8 minutes 46 seconds kneeling tributes, which came off as even more performative than the move by Congress. Even while some praised the gesture as a step by police toward taking accountability for their actions, the skepticism from people who didn't trust the kneeling officers' motives overwhelmed the optimism that it indicated any commitment to meaningful reform of policy or even behavior. The skepticism proved to be well founded based on other officers' responses to demonstrations around the country—at the height of the first week of nationwide protests, a group of police officers in Buffalo took a knee with demonstrators, and one day later, video surfaced of Buffalo police officers (it was never determined whether any of them had been kneelers) shoving a seventy-five-year-old man to the concrete sidewalk and walking past him as he lay bleeding, without offering any help. The police's version of the story, that the man had attacked them, was belied by the video. Later in the year, police in both Buffalo and nearby Rochester killed Black men who were experiencing mental-health episodes. In the Rochester incident, the man, Daniel Prude, died in part from the effects of officers pinning him to the ground until he lost consciousness.

The discordant images came from all over. Police kneeling in cities while their fellow officers were teargassing and tasing protesters elsewhere in the same city. Police kneeling while wearing riot gear, with armored vehicles nearby. Police kneeling early in the day, and law enforcement bringing helicopters to disperse crowds later. The ultimate show of hypocrisy came months later—in several cities, the same police departments in which officers showed public solidarity with those protesting against their tactics had officers travel to Washington to participate in the protests that led to the January 6 storming of the Capitol. Here, the officers who had previously signaled an understanding of the hurt, vulnerability, and need for change in the face of a constant threat to their lives that the citizens they served were expressing, in the hopes of inducing those same protestors to peaceful law and order, themselves turned around to support what would become a violent coup in defiance of a lawful democratic election for the purpose of maintaining the status quo.

Feeding the distrust—and directly sparking the confrontations between protestors and the police imported in huge numbers to suppress demonstrations—was the way that the investigation of Floyd's killing by Minneapolis city and county officials was handled early on. Residents demanded that Chauvin and his partners be brought to justice, but time dragged on, and by the fourth day after the video came out, the Hennepin County medical examiner had sent a message that the police were not going to be held responsible—and that Floyd himself would be held responsible instead.

The medical examiner's report reads:

The autopsy revealed no physical findings that support a diagnosis of traumatic asphyxia or strangulation. Mr. Floyd had underlying health conditions including coronary artery disease and hypertensive heart disease. The combined effects of Mr. Floyd being restrained by police, his underlying health conditions and any potential intoxicants in his system likely contributed to his death.

The official police statement released to the media, with the video already having made the rounds, only added to the fear of the police being absolved of all guilt. The headline on the statement read, "Man Dies after Medical Incident during Police Interaction."

Major League Soccer (MLS) returned in July from its pandemic pause. Its first games were in a bubble environment in Florida. The game between Orlando and Miami was played without spectators, with the people allowed on site comprising mostly the participants and the broadcast crew. They and the TV audience got to witness one of the first collective team and league demonstrations on behalf of Floyd—players wearing shirts with the names of victims, "Black Lives Matter" and other slogans, and combinations of names and messages demanding justice and humanity. Many of the players wore black gloves. The game did not begin with a playing of the national anthem. It did begin with the players lined up, in silence, either kneeling or standing with fists raised, for 8 minutes 46 seconds.

As play resumed around the league, teams also resumed playing the national anthem. Several players, sometimes entire teams, kneeled during the song—and where fans were allowed inside, several booed the gesture. Dallas and Nashville met in Frisco, Texas, and when the players kneeled before the game, boos rained down on them. In a postgame press conference, Reggie Cannon of Dallas, who is Black, returned the anger toward those fans:

> You got fans booing you for people taking a stand for what they believe in. Millions of other people support this cause and we discussed with every other team and the league what we're going to do and we've got fans booing us in our own stadium. How disgraceful is that? Honestly, for lack of a better word, it pissed me off.

In the climate of the growing movement, the athletes were losing the patience to calmly explain their positions, as Kaepernick had once upon a time.

Thierry Henry, one of the all-time greats as a player for France, who had become the MLS coach of Montreal, chose not to restrict his gesture to the pregame. Wearing a Black Lives Matter shirt and with his right fist raised, Henry took a knee for the first 8 minutes 46 seconds of his team's game against New England.

The U.S. Women's National Team chose this window, the aftermath of the Floyd killing, to change its rule banning kneeling by players during the anthem—the ban it had put in place four years earlier in response to Megan Rapinoe's supportive gesture for Kaepernick. The pandemic kept the team from returning to action until November . . . and when it did, against the Netherlands team that it had defeated in the World Cup final a year earlier, the players took a knee during the national anthem. They wore warmup jackets with "Black Lives Matter" inlaid across the front in red, white, and blue. The game took place after the presidential elections and after Joe Biden had been declared the winner over the national team's years-long nemesis, Trump.

The NBA that summer also chose to waive its policy requiring players to stand during the national anthem when they returned from the pandemic. It was an important concession and a win for the players, who had discussed collectively not returning to complete the season in light of the social climate. Kyrie Irving of the Brooklyn Nets was at the forefront of that discussion, and he opted out of the season—and created a fund to give financial help to WNBA players who had opted out of theirs. The clearest manifestation of the NBA's policy change was the team-wide kneeling before games.

That response was not unanimous, as team decisions to kneel generally have not been. Miami Heat center Meyers Leonard chose to stand with his hand over his heart as his teammates kneeled on either side of him. His explanation was a familiar one, used by opponents of the protests (Drew Brees, for example) as a purposeful misrepresentation of its stated intent: Citing his brother's deployment with the Marines in Afghanistan, he told the Associated Press, "I am with the Black Lives Matter movement and I love and support the military and my brother and the people who have fought to defend our rights in this country."

Leonard's explanation and motives were later called into more serious doubt and discredit the following season when, while on the Heat's injured list, he was overheard making an anti-Semitic slur ("fucking k—e bitch") during an online video game. He was fined $50,000 and suspended for a week by the team. He was also mercilessly dragged by players across the league, with several noting his refusal to kneel with his Black teammates the year before.

The dissension by Leonard came before the shooting of Blake. It was not necessarily forgotten when the league's play-off teams walked out. The strike reduced it largely to a footnote and an anomaly within the overwhelming statement that the NBA players made in sum through their actions in the bubble. The power exercised in the walkout was revelatory and far outstripped any statement made in the bubble before it: the most consequential job action that sports had seen since the labor strikes in pro sports decades earlier.

The magnitude of the walkout even made it easy to overlook James's statement in a game soon following the league's postpandemic return. In warmups for a Lakers game against the Toronto Raptors, James wore a T-shirt with "8:46" on the front.

The words and reactions from every other sport, athlete, and audience around the world, no matter how consequential, earthshaking, and conversation-shifting, all served to cast the public's attention toward how the NFL and its players would react. The league of Kaepernick—sitting on the bench, bending down on one knee, and then being banished from sight—would bring the entire movement full circle, thanks to the nine minutes or so of inhumanity in Minneapolis that had wound up being a fulfillment of the exiled quarterback's prophecy. "This is why they kneel" was designed to strike the NFL with full force.

The first NFL game months after the last 8 minutes 46 seconds of Floyd's life marked an indelible reminder of where the NFL had traveled since the early days of Kaepernick's protests . . . and how the public had largely run in place. That was the opening night of the 2020 season, the debut of the newly crowned Super Bowl champion Kansas City Chiefs, at home in a stadium with limited fan attendance due to the pandemic, against the Houston Texans. The NFL's nod to the times was visible on the backline of each end zone: the slogans "End Racism" and "It Takes All of Us." The visual of those phrases on the perimeter of the "Chiefs" printed in the end zone was fodder for widespread ridicule—it was the last team in the league still bearing a name and using a logo with Native American imagery, the nod to careless, nonchalant racism that the league felt in no rush to end. (To its credit, the owner in Washington had finally given in and removed the other, even more virulently offensive name, "Redskins," from his team after nearly ninety years, to be known for the time being as the Washington Football Team. The NFL didn't really play a role in that change, but at least it wasn't still defending its use as it had for years.)

The bigger issue that night was the gesture of unity among the players from both teams before kickoff, separate from the national anthem and anything connected to the flag. It was merely players linking arms. The fans booed it. It was another bracing wake-up call to all those who had hoped that Black lives really had begun to matter to the NFL's in-person paying audiences.

That was how the season began. Like the other sports, professional football had been disrupted by the pandemic, with the league's biggest casualty being the exhibition schedule. The annual NFL draft had actually benefited from its totally virtual format, making space for resourcefulness, authenticity, and a closer look into the lives and circumstances of the prospects as they celebrated in their homes among loved ones, maneuvering around the masking and distancing requirements.

Then Floyd's killing turned the league upside down . . . and set off one of the longest, most widespread, most sustained episodes of "We Tried to Tell You" ever witnessed. To borrow the analogy made so succinctly in a different era by Malcolm X after a different national tragedy, the NFL's chickens had come home to roost. The league that had pandered to the most hysterical, racist, ultra-right-wing, MAGA-loving segment of its audience; had indulged owners, executives, and coaches who tried to justify their prejudice in blackballing Kaepernick; and had tried to impose harsh penalties against any player who wanted to demand justice for the victims of police violence had to reckon with the fact that Kaepernick had been right all along in peacefully but conspicuously calling their attention to the vulnerability of his community at the hands of police brutality. They should have listened to and respected him.

A cross-section of NFL players—including the reigning Super Bowl Most Valuable Player (MVP), Patrick Mahomes—had posted a video the week of Floyd's killing, insisting that they "w[ould] not be silenced"; declaring, "I am George Floyd" and adding the many names of other victims of police violence; and telling the league to admit that it was wrong in how it had demonized player protest—and to say, loudly and unequivocally, that Black lives mattered. They also got in a dig at Brees, who that same week had issued his poorly timed declaration that he would never agree with kneeling.

The video put the league squarely on the spot. The league office and most of the teams had issued their boilerplate statements of sympathy for Floyd and for the divisiveness in the country and the need for unity. Not enough, the players said, not now, not after what you did these last four years. Say the words and say the names, they said.

The next day, commissioner Roger Goodell posted a video of his own and in eighty-one seconds said the words and named the names:

It has been a difficult time in our country, in particular, for Black people in our country. First, my condolences to the families of George Floyd, Breonna Taylor, Ahmaud Arbery, and all the families that have endured police brutality. We, the National Football League, condemn racism and the systematic oppression of Black people. We, the National Football League, admit we were wrong for not listening to NFL players earlier and encourage all to speak out and peacefully protest. We, the National Football League, believe Black Lives Matter. I personally protest with you and want to be a part of the much-needed change in this country. Without Black players, there would be no National Football League. And the protests around the country are emblematic of the centuries of silence, inequality, and oppression of Black players, coaches, fans, and staff. We are listening, I am listening, and I will be reaching out to players who have raised their voices and others on how we can move forward together for a better and more united NFL family.

It was a stunning acknowledgment and went far further than anyone who had followed the league in the previous five years had expected. With that, it never mentioned Kaepernick, his continued exile from the league, or any semblance of an apology to him. At the time of publication of this book, the NFL still had not offered an apology to Kaepernick, nor has any team attempted to sign him.

The NFL did, however, create a program to acknowledge the movement that it had gone through so much effort to ignore or erase. For the season, it allowed players to put on the back of their helmets the names of victims whom they wanted to honor and bring attention and awareness to throughout the season. Like the WNBA players with their jerseys bearing Breonna Taylor's name and Naomi Osaka's U.S. Open masks, this visual acknowledgment was a way to put the cost of racism and oppression in full view of everybody who could otherwise feign ignorance of the details. The NFL's marketing made sure that the names that players honored got all the publicity they could. The league posted videos of the names on the helmets and interviews with the players talking about their choices and telling the stories of the lives that had been lost.

Most of the names were already embedded in the national consciousness—Floyd, Taylor, Tamir Rice, Garner, Castile, and so many others. Some players took advantage of the moment to shed light on many who had gone overlooked or had fallen through the cracks of exposure. At least three players, including Kenny Stills, a player who had begun kneeling as Kaepernick had early on and continued over the years with different teams, chose Vanessa Guillen, a twenty-year-old soldier at Ft. Hood who was murdered in 2020 by another soldier stationed with her. Two others paid tribute to India Kager, a Navy veteran shot to death in 2015 by Virginia Beach police who fired into the car she was driving, aiming at a man in the passenger seat. Three players chose Sharonda Coleman Singleton, one of the nine victims of the massacre in a Charleston, South Carolina, church by white supremacist Dylann Roof in 2015.

DeAndre Hopkins, then of the Houston Texans, made a unique choice, someone executed by the authorities some two centuries before the other victims memorialized. Hopkins, it is worth recalling, was the most demonstrative player following the incident where owner Bob McNair had been quoted calling the players "inmates" running the "prison." Hopkins also had spoken on the video scolding the NFL and shaming Goodell into his apology. The name that Hopkins wore was Denmark Vesey—the former slave from South Carolina, Hopkins's home state, who organized a slave rebellion and was discovered, arrested, and hanged on July 2, 1822. Vesey also was a co-founder of the African Methodist Episcopalian Church in Charleston, best known as Mother Emanuel . . . the church in which Roof had murdered Singleton and eight other Black worshippers that day in 2015.

The NFL's skeptical Black stakeholders and audience, hoping that such a powerful institution so dependent on Black talent (and suffering, through the sport's inherent violence) was indeed honest about undertaking such an unprecedented commitment to a change in American life, scrutinized such gestures for superficiality, with concerns that the establishments making them were doing the bare minimum required without instituting systemic change and truly committing to antiracism. The NFL certainly appeared to fall into that category in light of its continued blackballing of Kaepernick and its incapability of hiring Black coaches and executives, but the helmet gesture still was significant relative to what it had done before.

Naturally, a few players decided not to play along, instead committing themselves to using their platform to undermine the very motivation of the Black Lives Matter movement: the vulnerability of America's Black citizens at the hands of those social structures charged with protecting all Americans. Steelers tackle Alejandro Villanueva fit that category. He had already sought to undermine his teammates' statement during the national anthem before a 2017 game, after they had agreed to stay in the locker room as a statement against Trump and his insults. Now, Villanueva separated himself again after teammates had agreed to all wear the name of Antwon Rose Jr., a Black teenager killed by police in Pittsburgh in 2018. Villanueva decided to wear the name Alwyn Cashe, a Black soldier recently killed in action in Iraq—rationalizing his choice by claiming that the Black Lives Matter movement was being selective about which lives actually mattered to it. It was, again, not an original rebuttal to the movement by people who were devoted to silencing it and one that denied the unique vulnerability that the movement highlighted from the American state itself. Michelle Kenney, Rose's mother, praised the Steelers for coming to her with their idea to honor her son—and also scorched Villanueva for rejecting the idea and going out of his way to avoid it. "I have nothing against vets and absolutely appreciate everything that they have done and continue to do for us," Kenney's social media post read. "But this one person showed us exactly who he is and obviously he didn't approve of how the vote turned out."

A similar tactic was employed by Tyler Eifert, tight end for the Jacksonville Jaguars, who, in the midst of a league-wide, sports-wide, nationwide, and worldwide reckoning with a culture of police treating Black people indecently and inhumanely, chose to honor a Black police officer, David Dorn. The retired Dorn had been slain in the summer of 2020 when he answered an alarm at a pawn shop in the vicinity of the social justice protests in St. Louis. Right-wing provocateurs immediately seized upon his slaying and claimed that he was killed during the protest violence, even though no ties between the protests and his killing were ever established. It was a clear disinformation campaign designed to, again, discredit the movement with a tag of "hypocrisy." Eifert went to the trouble of extending it to the NFL.

The resistance of 2020 in the league of Kaepernick inspired a resistance of its own. The defense of the system that made Kaepernick an outcast, took his livelihood from him, protected the paying public and employees who cherished white supremacy, and, eventually, choked the life out of Floyd, was not going to buckle easily.

But there was no longer a doubt about why anybody kneeled.

THE ROAD FROM PARIAH TO ICON

One of the popular opinions about Colin Kaepernick's motivation for his protest during the 49ers' exhibition games in 2016 was that he was desperately grasping for relevancy. He was coming off the bench for a team that he had once led to a Super Bowl. He had fallen down the depth chart and fallen out of favor. He was pretty close to being washed up. He was about to get cut. He would be out of the league before much longer. He had to call attention to himself somehow. Disrespecting the troops, the flag, the national anthem, and this country and everything it stood for, especially after everything it had done for him, and daring to claim that it was because of racism, when his biracial self was making $12 million a year? Of course that's why he was doing it. Give this stunt a few weeks, this line of thinking went, and nobody will ever hear from him again.

Fast forward five years, to the spring of 2021. Former Heisman Trophy winner, former NFL starting quarterback, former journeyman, former minor-league baseball player, and former college football broadcaster Tim Tebow was about to get another National Football League (NFL) opportunity. His old college coach, Urban Meyer, wanted to give him a look with his new NFL team, the Jacksonville Jaguars, back in Tebow's home state, where he'll be a hero forever. Tebow would get a look at tight end, a position that he had never played. He had not been in so much as an NFL training camp in six years and had not played in an NFL game that counted in eight.

Wait, came the reply from a vast swath of America. He can get another chance to play in the NFL six years removed from football, and Kaepernick, after just five years, can't? Also, have you squeezed in an apology to Kaepernick since you hoisted the banner of "Black Lives Matter" last year?

Wait yourself, came the reply from another vast swath. What does that guy have to do with this? Are we still talking about Kaepernick?

They were still talking about Kaepernick. Contrary to that very popular prediction in the late summer of 2016, America never stopped talking about him. The world never stopped talking about him. It is extremely difficult to imagine him ever being forgotten. He is now eternally part of the conversation that includes Muhammad Ali, Tommie Smith and John Carlos, Bill Russell, Jackie Robinson, Jack Johnson, and so many others. The story of the NFL can't be told without him anymore. Neither can the story of civil rights; of human rights; of American history; of Black American history; of revolution and protest and resistance; of systemic, structural, and fundamental change; of reweaving the fabric of society; of redefining rights, citizenship, and freedom. Possibly even the history of the end of policing as this nation has always known it, or maybe for good.

Those possibilities are far into the future, but others are close enough for the current generation to see. There is no longer any doubt that Kaepernick lit a flame that nobody has been able to put out, even while his career in the sport he played, excelled in, and committed himself to was extinguished.

Along the way, he collected his share of accolades and honors—not for the football career that ended at age twenty-nine but for everything he did while enduring his exile. He was named to *TIME* magazine's list of 100 Most Influential People. He earned *Sports Illustrated*'s Muhammad Ali Legacy Award. He was anointed *GQ*'s Citizen of the Year and Amnesty International's Ambassador of Conscience. Harvard University presented him with its W. E. B. Du Bois Medal. A citation about Kaepernick's "unforgivable Blackness" would have been fitting for this honor.

For the first few years that he spent in the spotlight, he existed at this level of consciousness and awareness while barely speaking. He did not make speeches, and while he maximized social media as an avenue of communication, he used it to get information about his causes out rather than to engage constantly with either his supporters or his detractors.

For the next few years, he found more ways to tell his story. Eventually, he formed his own media company and announced plans to produce a memoir. He also confirmed plans for a documentary series about his youth and the influences that brought him to this point, in collaboration with award-winning director Ava DuVernay. By late in 2020, casting had begun for the reenactments of those earlier stages in his life, with actors picked to portray his teenage self. The series, *Colin in Black & White*, debuted on the Netflix streaming service in October 2021. He also signed with Disney to develop scripted and nonscripted work.

The Know Your Rights Camps that so many discovered when he began kneeling continued to expand to other sites and reach other populations. The organization started in the San Francisco Bay Area but was in six more markets by the time the reckoning over George Floyd was underway. Kaepernick regularly appeared in person at the various camps, speaking and being hands-on with the participants, and he always drew supporters who aligned with his philosophy and had already embedded themselves in those communities. Plans were announced for two more publications under his brand. One was an anthology that he would edit of works by an all-star lineup of rights advocates and activists, distributed through the Know Your Rights Camp. *Abolition for the People:*

The Movement for a Future without Policing and Prisons went on sale in October 2021. He also authored a children's book about self-identity based on his life growing up, titled *I Color Myself Differently*, to be published in the spring of 2022.

Yet Kaepernick himself moved under the radar, showing up with little or no fanfare and often not being noticed in a location until the camp's social media sites posted photos and clips of his appearances with the youngsters and organizers. His stealthy travels made his meetings with, for example, Smith and Carlos, separately, all the more effective. The people he needed to be around got access to him one way or another.

Kaepernick often let the Know Your Rights Camp's social media sites, and his most ardent supporters, pass his messages around. On his own sites, he was as selective as could be, weighing in when it would have the most impact. On the dates that honored Robinson—the annual celebration of the anniversary of his major-league debut and the recognition in 2019 of the hundredth anniversary of his birth—Kaepernick posted about Robinson and his comments from his autobiography, about no longer wanting to stand for the national anthem in light of what a lifetime as a Black American had taught him. Kaepernick did not let the continued police brutality against Black people go unnoticed, nor did he miss an opportunity to comment on how police were, or were not, held accountable. When Minnesota policeman Jeronimo Yanez was acquitted in 2017 of murder charges for killing Philando Castile, Kaepernick posted well-known side-by-side photos of a modern police badge and a historic slave patrol badge, adding: "You Can't Ignore Your History . . . Always Remember Who You Are."

His post in late May 2020, as the rage over Floyd's killing was peaking, read:

When civility leads to death, revolting is the only logical reaction. The cries for peace will rain down, and when they do, they will land on deaf ears, because your violence has brought this resistance. We have the right to fight back! Rest in Power George Floyd

Inversely, when Derek Chauvin was convicted on murder charges the following year, a tidal wave of reactions mentioned Kaepernick's name, tied together by the theme, "He was right."

Time has continued to prove him, his actions, and his strategic decisions to be correct. The NFL players who came together in 2020 to call out Roger Goodell and the league did so with Kaepernick's actions in mind—and even though Goodell failed to apologize to Kaepernick, the power of seeing him say, "We were wrong," was undeniable.

For certain, the verdict against Chauvin, or the year of activism that preceded it, did not change every heart and mind, not even in sports overall or in the NFL specifically. Drew Brees proved that. So did the handful of players who openly rebelled against the NFL's program to use helmet messages to honor Black people victimized by white terrorism and violence. So did retired Hall of Fame quarterback Brett Favre. In the week before the verdict, Favre had gone onto a radio show and declared that he did not want sports to be interrupted by outside factors anymore:

> I know when I turn on a game, I want to watch a game. I want to watch players play and teams win, lose, come from behind. I want to watch all the important parts of the game, not what's going on outside of the game, and I think the general fan feels the same way. I can't tell you how many people have said to me, "I don't watch anymore; it's not about the game anymore." And I tend to agree.

After the guilty verdict, Favre went onto his podcast and said, "I find it hard to believe, and I'm not defending Derek Chauvin in any way, I find it hard to believe, first of all, that he intentionally meant to kill George Floyd."

At the same time, many of the people who had studiously distanced themselves from Kaepernick's stance and the NFL's aggressive campaign to silence him and the players remained silent during this clear-cut justification of everything Kaepernick had done. Nothing particularly definitive or memorable about the Chauvin verdict came out of Cam Newton, or Dak Prescott, or Jerry Rice, or Jim Brown, or Ray Lewis, or any of the multitudes of people who either sold the unity line or declared that Kaepernick had nothing to complain about—or needed to find a more acceptable way to complain.

Kaepernick himself did not join the "I Told You So" chorus, not in any great volume, at least. He was very strategic in picking his spots. Three years after signing a Nike endorsement deal in 2018 that raised questions about whether he had chosen the most effective method of promoting his cause—or, worse, whether he had turned the cause into a giant shoe commercial—his initial campaign still packed a punch and could stand on its own as justifying his choice. It still attracts enormous traffic online, it has been hailed as a landmark in social justice cause marketing, and it earned a Creative Arts Emmy award for the best commercial of the year. Among all the images on display, two lines he narrated jump out to define the message: "Believe in something, even if it means sacrificing everything" and "Don't ask if your dreams are crazy, ask if they're crazy enough."

Along with that, he has had a handful of limited releases of branded apparel that always sell out fast, shoes and shirts and jerseys with his uniform No. 7 on them. Since he has not played any football since 2016, when he started in eleven games for a team that won two games all season and cleaned house from top to bottom afterward, the allure clearly is his association with commitment and conviction to one's ideals. Related to the sales for his apparel company, however, his 49ers jersey has been on sale through the team and NFL shops since the season he spent protesting, and it has continued to sell well, even with the team turning around and reaching the Super Bowl three seasons after his last snap for them.

The NFL's attempts to forget him and nudge the public toward forgetting him carried on right up until the Floyd killing, and the public reaction to it shook the league to its core. That Super Bowl after the 2019 season was the best and most recent proof. The 49ers' rebirth as contenders meant that, on the surface, ignoring Kaepernick would be impossible. He, the 2016 season, and the organizational purge that followed were an essential part of the narrative of their return to the Super Bowl. He represented the only moment of true success it had had in the previous quarter century, since the end of the Joe Montana–Steve Young glory years. He had been the quarterback who took them to the Super Bowl after the 2012 season. He had taken them to the NFC championship game the following year. He had set an NFL postseason single-game record for quarterbacks, and an overall 49ers postseason record, for rushing yards in an other-worldly performance in Lambeau Field in a playoff win over the Packers that season. He had been part of the fall, a pawn in the feud between coach Jim Harbaugh and owner Jed York. His production had fallen, he had survived two coaching changes and a season cut short by injury, and then the team had fallen off a cliff at the same time he had begun to kneel before games and shine a light on a national crisis. The franchise had gone down, then up, then down, then up again, and Kaepernick had been along for the ride as one of the lead actors in every chapter.

Yet it became clear during the National Football Conference (NFC) championship game against Green Bay that year, and in the two-week buildup to the Super Bowl against the Kansas City Chiefs, that Kaepernick had been erased in the universe of the 49ers and the NFL. His name was never mentioned by the networks covering the games. In the Packers game itself, Raheem Mostert set a new franchise play-off rushing record with 196 yards. As he approached the record, when he broke it, and afterward, the network broadcasting the game, Fox, never spoke or posted a graphic with the former record-holder's name. As for the two weeks of hype and then the actual game day, if Kaepernick's name ever got mentioned, it never stuck in anybody's memory.

In defense of the league, Kaepernick's presence was felt in that Super Bowl, during the halftime show featuring Jennifer Lopez and Shakira. The entertainment was the visible manifestation of the partnership formed earlier that year between the NFL and the entertainment mogul Jay-Z, an initiative labeled "Inspire Change." Label this, however, a facetious defense. From its inception, "Inspire Change" gave off the aroma of a plot to pacify Black voices who had been shouting for genuine fundamental change in how the NFL was addressing not only the problems that Kaepernick had called attention to with his protests but also the problems of players who continued to protest against the will of the owners, certain fans, and the routinely obstinate president. Incorporating Jay-Z and his automatic credibility gave the appearance of a league that wanted to listen. Jay-Z's own words gave the appearance that he had traded off access to the most lucrative and powerful sports league in America for the players' freedom and Kaepernick's future as a player. On the day that Goodell, the commissioner, and Jay-Z jointly announced their plans, Jay-Z said in language that would seem hard to misinterpret: "I think we've moved past kneeling. I think it's time for action." Given a chance to elaborate months later, before that Super Bowl, he said of Kaepernick to the *New York Times*: "No one is saying he hasn't been done wrong. He was done wrong. I would understand if it was three months ago. But it was three years ago and someone needs to say, 'What do we do now—because people are still dying?'"

More than a year passed after that observation, and it was hard to see what the NFL was doing, and had planned to do, before it was carried along in the momentum of the movement after Floyd was killed.

The only thing that the NFL had appeared to do regarding the specific issue of giving Kaepernick a chance to play in the league again was to use his desire to return against him and try to manipulate him into giving up his right to sue the league. Afterward, Kaepernick's naysayers always tried to claim that the NFL gave him a chance to try out for its teams and he threw it away and burned a sincerely constructed bridge back into the league. Yet there was no doubt once the tryout was over that there was nothing sincere about it.

Out of nowhere in November 2019—his third year out of the NFL—Kaepernick got an invitation to a tryout at the Falcons' team facility in the Atlanta area. Teams rearranged their schedules to get a representative to the workout, some taking it more seriously and sending higher-ranking executives than others. But as the time of the workout neared, the league made Kaepernick's signing a liability waiver assuming responsibility for any injuries sustained in the workout—one that appeared slanted heavily in favor of the NFL and against Kaepernick—a condition of the workout. Kaepernick and his team refused. They quickly arranged a workout of their own about an hour from the original location. Several teams used that as an excuse not to attend, on the pretext that they could not reach the location or were on too tight a schedule to account for the change in plans, indicating that they had never taken it seriously enough to devote time or resources to seeing and evaluating him. Kaepernick went ahead and worked out anyway, had it recorded for teams who might want to see it, and arranged for it to be streamed. It didn't stop the quick reply from those opposing him—that he had been offered a tryout and had turned it down. Everything about it came off like a sham, a setup to actually put the possibility of him returning to play to a permanent halt.

When the tryout was over and he took a rare opportunity to speak to the reporters who had attended the workout, he talked like a man who had figured out in advance that the NFL wasn't above board. "We are waiting for the thirty-two owners, thirty-two teams, and Roger Goodell to stop running. Stop running from the truth, stop running from the people. We are ready to play. We are ready to go anywhere," he said.

He was never signed or contacted by any team for the rest of that season, the year after, and the off-season that followed that.

Still, at the first Super Bowl after the racial and social reckoning brought about by Floyd's murder, as the NFL figured out what "We were wrong" meant in the broad context of its public image, Kaepernick's image made appearances that just a year earlier would have been impossible to imagine.

One image was on a mural in Tampa, related to the campaign by Ben & Jerry's around the ice cream flavor dedicated to him and around the causes that he represented and to which he had committed himself.

The other was in a video produced by the NFL and CBS for the Super Bowl pregame show, just under seven minutes long, narrated by Oscar-winning actress Viola Davis. It was a lesson in the history of Black players in the NFL, from its roots, to its abrupt segregation in 1933, to its reintegration in 1946, and the role in that history of one of the players integrating it—Kenny Washington, of the Rams team who had promised to integrate so that the city government of Los Angeles would allow it to play there. The closing montage of images was accompanied by these words from Davis:

> This is what led us to Doug Williams. This is what got us to Tony Dungy and Ozzie Newsome. This is what gave us Marlin Briscoe, Jim Brown, Walter Payton, and all the Black players who defied the odds, inspiring those who make the National Football League look like the nation it represents today.

It could not have fit the current times better, and it reflected exceedingly well on the NFL, which can never be accused of telling its greatest stories poorly or inadequately. This time, though, its story was more complete than it ever had been, because with less than a minute left in the piece, amid the shots of Brown and Payton and Rice and Barry Sanders, was a brief highlight of Kaepernick, racing past a tackler. It was jarring, not because it was unfamiliar or because it reminded all of how recently he had been pulling off moves like that. It was because it was a brief reprieve from the erasure. Kaepernick had not been neatly snipped out of the history of the sport and the memories of its followers, not edited out as his name had been from the soundtrack of the Madden video game package in 2018, only to be edited back in when the backlash came hard and fast. The 2012 and 2013 seasons and postseasons weren't a figment of anyone's imagination after all. There had been a Super Bowl for the 49ers that didn't include Montana, Young, or Jimmy Garoppolo. Someone had held the franchise record for play-off rushing yards before Mostert had—the listing in the record books did not read "Vacated."

How much had Kaepernick been deleted? The Ben & Jerry's mural in Tampa was not the first to honor him at the NFL's showcase event. One had been created for him in Atlanta in 2017, by local artist Fabian Williams, rendering him as a member of the Falcons (even wearing Michael Vick's old number, 7, which the two share) and standing next to Ali. The week of the Super Bowl festivities for the 2019 game, between the New England Patriots and Los Angeles Rams, the building was torn down.

Said Williams to the *Atlanta Journal-Constitution*: "I figured at some point they would tear the building down, but it has been sitting up this whole time. The fact that the Super Bowl happens here and the weekend when the festivities are gearing up, the building gets demolished is very odd."

The tug of war between those who revered Kaepernick and what he stood, sat, and kneeled for and those who wanted every trace of his existence removed from public life was destined to continue. It was interrupted, and the direction altered, only by one of the most heinous crimes the world had been exposed to up close. If Floyd's execution by Chauvin and his partners had not been preserved by a camera phone, the reckoning might never have taken place, the proof of Kaepernick's point would never have been showered across every screen, and the NFL would never have been moved to get the commissioner to look into his own phone camera and hold himself and his owner bosses accountable for their actions. And Kaepernick would not have made the final cut of the NFL's version of history. The video might not ever have been made. The league certainly had never been in the "lionize Kenny Washington" business or the business of asking Davis to lend it some of her credibility. They were not far removed from writing a large check to Jay-Z for his credibility.

In the beginning, when Kaepernick's kneeling was dismissed as a cry for help to save his sinking career, it also was ridiculed as an act that should never be mentioned in the same wing of the library as Ali or Smith and Carlos, never mind the same breath. Plenty saw the gravity of the times and recognized the validity of the comparison, but they were largely the same people who had intimately felt the pain and anguish of the murders of Castile and Alton Sterling, could relate to Kaepernick's anguish—and did not need to see the slaying of men in uniform in Texas to move them to suddenly beg for an end to the violence and the lack of love and respect for our fellow Americans. Sterling and Castile, they believed, were Americans worthy of just as much love and respect and safety from violence as those officers. Kaepernick had been courageous enough to say it and then to put his career on the line to try to achieve it. It was convincing enough to talk about him as a hero whose spirit had been shared by the Alis five decades earlier. To the rest, he was Public Enemy No. 1, and he had to be balled up and thrown away as a lesson to anyone and everyone else who might start thinking and acting like him.

That all raises the likelihood that some day—not now, with the forces of white supremacy willing to fight to the death to defend themselves against the threat that he represents, but some time well into the future—Kaepernick will be hailed as a hero. Exactly the way that Ali, the most despised man in America in the late 1960s and 1970s but beloved enough to light the Olympic torch on U.S. soil in the 1990s, became a hero. The way that Smith and Carlos, who had to watch their backs as they crossed the San José State campus for classes after returning from Mexico City for fear of being shot dead along the way, had a statue dedicated to them, had another placed in the Smithsonian's National Museum of African American History and Culture, were admitted into the U.S. Olympic Hall of Fame fifty-two years after they won their medals . . . and were invited to the White House by President Barack Obama.

Dr. Glenn Bracey, a Villanova sociology professor, finds it all hilarious and hopes that someone in fifty years will make sure to remind those who elevate Kaepernick onto a pedestal of the truth of his day: "Hey, y'all wouldn't let that man work. Stop it, stop it, stop it."

To Bracey, the enduring problem for every moment that Black people have been on this continent, and certainly throughout the century-plus of Black people on the stage of sports, is the need for the nation to claim victories and present itself with rewards for ensuring that overall, everything remains exactly as it was intended. "People are so invested in this notion of progress," he told the *Sporting News*. "I know what you really believe when I look at your opposition to protest being the exact same in 2018 as it was 1968. That's not progress. We're in the same place."

The story of Kaepernick was the same from 2016 to the summer of 2020. What happened after that is hard to define as progress. What it looks like in 2066 might look that way, but another iteration of Floyd's public death at the hands of people sworn to protect him would make that a lie.

If or when that happens—if or when the current reckoning is beaten back, physically, as the rioters of January 6 in the Capitol Building tried to do—there might be a statue of Kaepernick somewhere, maybe even in many places, for onlookers to gather under, to feel his inspiration and absorb that spirit and find inspiration to make sure that the enemy never gets comfortable.

Just like there was in 2020, when people decided that the world had to change, and they decided that one inspirational place to gather and plan and embrace each other and work toward a future of freedom, equality, and justice for all . . . was under the statue on San José State's campus of Smith and Carlos.

Whether the resisters of the world congregate beneath a statue of Prescott, or Jimmie Hines, or even Michael Jordan or Tiger Woods or Jay-Z, remains to be seen.

EPILOGUE

The biggest-name competitor at the USA Track & Field Golden Games at Mt. San Antonio College in May 2021 was actually a 230-pound NFL wide receiver. At least that was the main draw for a national television audience and numerous news outlets on a Sunday afternoon in northern California—Seattle Seahawks wide receiver DK Metcalf was adding competition in the 100-meter dash at a prelude to the U.S. Olympic trials to his off-season training regimen.

Still, the most dedicated track and field fans were planning to look beyond the men's 100 heats and toward the finals that featured the nation's true Olympic hopefuls. They included Noah Lyles, one of the best in the world at 200 meters. The twenty-three-year-old native of the Washington, D.C., suburb of Alexandria, Virginia, was the reigning world champion, and while he was a threat for gold in the 100 meters and a candidate for the 4 × 100 relay at the upcoming Games in Tokyo, the 200 was his event. But as the years passed beyond his 2019 world championship win in Qatar, Lyles had begun to think about much bigger struggles than his own personal quest for additional gold.

The tipping point for him, as it was for the rest of the country and the world, was the George Floyd killing by police in Minneapolis in 2020. Lyles took to his social media to express his thoughts—and began by coming to grips with who the person was expressing them and why anyone should pay attention:

> There is so much I want to say but it's hard because all the positions I am in. But at a certain point you just have to say forget it because people need to see they have support. It hurts my heart because as an athlete I love running for my country. But as a Human being it is disheartening to know that my people are being killed while I go out and win metals [sic] for them to try and make the US look good.

It could have been lifted from a speech by athletes in 1968 and transported fifty-three years into the future. Or it could have been transmitted back to 1968 and handed to the leaders of the movement. Decades of activist athletes on the world stage, wearing "USA" across their chests, performing and winning for their country, wondering what that country truly thought of them, knowing that he would soon hear that he owed that country his gratitude and submission, while in fact it was the country that owed him and his people something much more fundamental.

Lyles kept training, kept running, kept preparing for what might be his once-in-a-lifetime moment, the urgency of it growing when the 2020 Games were postponed for a year by the COVID-19 pandemic. He also kept talking and even marched a few times in support of the Black Lives Matter movement.

And he decided to add a piece to his outfit for competition. Ato Boldon, the Olympic sprinter-turned-broadcaster, noticed it as Lyles settled into the blocks for the 200-meter final in the Golden Games.

It was a black glove on Lyles's left hand.

"If you know, Mexico City, 1968, Tommie Smith and John Carlos," Boldon informed the TV audience as the starting gun sounded.

Lyles chased down fellow American Kenny Bednarek in the last five meters to win. It was the second time that he had worn the glove in a major competition in the past year . . . and the second time that he had won.

The International Olympic Committee (IOC) had instituted a ban on athlete protests for the Tokyo Games—gestures on the medals stand, wearing gear supporting the likes of Black Lives Matter. As Lyles crossed the finish line at Mt. San Antonio College two months before the opening ceremonies in Tokyo, it was not clear whether the IOC would consider a black glove on the fist of a Black American running the 200 meters to be in violation of their rules.

From his platform, Lyles was willing to find out.

ACKNOWLEDGMENTS

The seeds for this book grew from my previous book, *Silent Gesture*, and its subject, Tommie Smith. When he and his wonderful wife and partner, Delois, allowed me to help tell his story back in the early 2000s, we knew that his story and his legacy would continue long after publication. The fiftieth anniversary of the stance that he and John Carlos took in Mexico City, in 2018, was the ideal time and place to revisit what he did and why it still stood the test of time.

The story for the *Sporting News* that October—"An Endless Fight, a Defining Choice"—grew from that seed. Thanks to Shaun Koiner, then the chief product and content officer, for suggesting the idea, supporting it, and accentuating the meaning and value of it to the entire company. Thanks as well to Tadd Haislop, who as an NFL editor found a way to give me the space to take on the project for more than a year amid the coverage of two NFL seasons and a full off-season . . . both of which, of course, featured the blackballed Colin Kaepernick as a main character. Jason Foster was the editor who saw the early drafts and encouraged the shifts in emphasis and injection of my personal interpretations of the history that I was detailing, which led to the centering of "choice" in the narrative.

So many significant figures in this story gave of their time to be interviewed for the original story and, by extension, this book, including Dr. Glenn Bracey, Jamal Henderson, Kenneth Shropshire, Toni Smith-Thompson, Tanisha Wright, and, again, Dr. Tommie Smith.

Years ago, Kevin Blackistone, whom I cherish as a fellow journalist, role model, and friend, introduced me to literary agent Brian Wood for another potential project. That one never came to fruition, but a personal and professional bond developed. It was Brian who asked in late 2020—as the social reckoning emerged in the wake of the police murder of George Floyd—whether I believed that I had a book idea that could put the movement into context. "An idea like the choice that athletes must make about using their platforms in the service of freedom and justice?" I replied.

The publishers that stepped up for *Silent Gesture* when none other would—Temple University Press—stepped up again. My eternal gratitude to those who helped bring Tommie Smith's story to print and picked up right where they had left off for this story, including Ann-Marie Anderson and Gary Kramer, and to those whom I met on this journey who helped make this a reality, including Ryan Mulligan, Ashley Petrucci, and Heather Wilcox.

Thank you to the universe of friends, colleagues, loved ones, and family who had my back during a time when I wasn't sure whether I had a project like this in me. Above them all are the two most important people in my life, now, then, and forever. Alexa and Renard, this is for you.

BIBLIOGRAPHY

Books

Carlos, John, with Dave Zirin. *The John Carlos Story*. Chicago: Haymarket Books, 2011.

Hietala, Thomas R. *The Fight of the Century: Jack Johnson, Joe Louis, and the Struggle for Racial Equality*. Armonk, NY: M. E. Sharpe, 2002.

Hodges, Craig, with Rory Fanning. *Long Shot: The Triumphs and Struggles of an NBA Freedom Fighter*. Chicago: Haymarket Books, 2017.

Kriegel, Mark. *Pistol: The Life of Pete Maravich*. New York: Free Press, 2007.

Mead, Chris. *Champion: Joe Louis, Black Hero in White America*. New York: Penguin, 1985.

Meggyesy, Dave. *Out of Their League*. Lincoln: University of Nebraska Press, 1970.

Murphy, Frank. *The Last Protest: Lee Evans in Mexico City*. Kansas City, MO: WindSprint Press, 2006.

Pluto, Terry. *Tall Tales: The Glory Years of the NBA, in the Words of the Men Who Played, Coached, and Built Pro Basketball*. New York: Simon and Schuster, 1992.

Remnick, David. *King of the World*. New York: Vintage Books, 1998.

Robertson, Oscar. *The Big O: My Life, My Times, My Game*. Emmaus, PA: Rodale, 2003.

Robinson, Jackie, as told to Alfred Duckett. *I Never Had It Made*. New York: Putnam, 1972.

Smith, Tommie, with David Steele. *Silent Gesture: The Autobiography of Tommie Smith*. Philadelphia: Temple University Press, 2007.

Thomas, Ron. *They Cleared the Lane: The NBA's Black Pioneers*. Lincoln: University of Nebraska Press, 2002.

Ward, Geoffrey C. *Unforgivable Blackness: The Rise and Fall of Jack Johnson*. New York: Alfred A. Knopf, 2005.

Articles

Associated Press. "Rodgers Throws TD Pass to Lead Packers Past 49ers 21-10." *ESPN*, August 27, 2016. https://www.espn.com/nfl/recap?gameId=400874788.

Axthelm, Pete. "Boycott Now—Boycott Later?" Vault, *Sports Illustrated*, February 26, 1968. https://vault.si.com/vault/1968/02/26/boycott-now-boycott-later.

Bieler, Des. "Bill Russell Led an NBA Boycott in 1961. Now He's Saluting Others for 'Getting in Good Trouble.'" *Washington Post*, August 27, 2020. https://www.washingtonpost.com/sports/2020/08/27/bill-russell-nba-boycott/.

Bogage, Jacob. "When A's Bruce Maxwell Knelt during the Anthem, His College Coach Disagreed. Then They Talked." *Washington Post*, September 24, 2017. https://www.washingtonpost.com/news/sports/wp/2017/09/24/when-as-bruce-maxwell-knelt-during-the-anthem-his-college-coach-disagreed-then-they-talked/.

Bontemps, Tim. "Michael Jordan Stands Firm on 'Republicans Buy Sneakers, Too' Quote, Says It Was Made in Jest." *ESPN*, May 4, 2020. https://www.espn.com/nba/story/_/id/29130478/michael-jordan-stands-firm-republicans-buy-sneakers-too-quote-says-was-made-jest.

Boren, Cindy, and Des Bieler. "'We Have Everything That I Like': Trump Serves Fast-Food Feast for Clemson's White House Visit." *Washington Post*, January 15, 2019. https://www.washingtonpost.com/sports/2019/01/14/clemson-tigers-visit-white-house-meet-with-trump/.

Davis, Amira Rose. "Sixty Years Ago She Refused to Stand for the Anthem." *ZORA*, September 26, 2019. https://zora.medium.com/sixty-years-ago-she-refused-to-stand-for-the-anthem-cf443b4e75c7.

Dougherty, Jesse. "Sean Doolittle on Declining White House Invite: 'I Don't Want to Hang Out with Somebody Who Talks Like That.'" *Washington Post*, November 2, 2019. https://www.washingtonpost.com/sports/2019/11/01/sean-doolittle-declining-white-house-invite-i-dont-want-hang-out-with-somebody-who-talks-like-that/.

Emanuel Nine Memorial. "Denmark Vesey—A Fighter for Racial Equality." Emanuel Nine Memorial, July 2, 2020. https://emanuelnine.org/2020/07/02/denmark-vesey-a-fighter-for-racial-equality/.

ESPN News Services. "Players Send Passionate Video Message to NFL about Racial Inequality." *ESPN*, June 5, 2020. https://www.espn.com/nfl/story/_/id/29269531/players-send-passionate-video-message-nfl-racial-inequality.

Fletcher, Michael A. "A Tearful Tiger Gets Honor of a Lifetime from a Controversial President." *The Undefeated*, May 6, 2019. https://theundefeated.com/features/tiger-woods-gets-medal-of-freedom-from-president-trump/.

Given, Karen, and Shira Springer. "Before Kaepernick, the 'Syracuse 8' Were Blackballed by Pro Football." *WBUR*, November 17, 2017. https://www.wbur.org/onlyagame/2017/11/17/syracuse-8-football-boycott-kaepernick.

Goff, Steven. "With Raised Fists, a Moment of Silence and BLM Shirts, MLS's Troubled Restart Officially Opens." *Washington Post*, July 8, 2020. https://www.washingtonpost.com/sports/2020/07/08/mls-makes-its-troubled-return-orlando-city-inter-miami-open-league-tournament/.

Hardman, A. L. "Baylor's Refusal to Play Here Brings ABC Protest." *Charleston Gazette-Mail*, January 18, 1959. https://archive.wvculture.org/history/africanamericans/baylor03.html.

Hartman, Sid. "Back in 1959, Minneapolis Lakers Star Elgin Baylor Refused to Play to Protest Racism." *Star Tribune*, August 28, 2020. https://www.startribune.com/hartman-in-1959-lakers-star-baylor-refused-to-play-to-protest-racism/572245502/.

Jones, Mike. "Legalese, Mistrust and Late Negotiating: How Colin Kaepernick and the NFL Broke Apart on Workout." *USA Today*, November 21, 2019. https://www.usatoday.com/story/sports/nfl/2019/11/21/colin-kaepernick-nfl-workout-waiver-teams-quarterback/4259272002/.

Kilgore, Adam. "Noah Lyles Runs for His Country, and He Wants to Help Make It Better." *Washington Post*, June 6, 2020. https://www.washingtonpost.com/sports/2020/06/06/noah-lyles-runs-his-country-he-wants-help-make-it-better/.

———. "Noah Lyles's Latest Win Comes with a Salute to Tommie Smith and John Carlos." *Washington Post*, August 14, 2020. https://www.washingtonpost.com/sports/2020/08/14/noah-lyles-win-tommie-smith-john-carlos/.

Klores, Dan. "Blackballing in the NBA Kept Cleo Hill from Becoming a Star." *The Undefeated*, October 25, 2018. https://theundefeated.com/features/blackballing-in-the-nba-kept-cleo-hill-from-becoming-a-star/.

Lowery, Wesley, and Jacob Bogage. "Fifty Years after the 'Black 14' Were Banished, Wyoming Football Reckons with the Past." *Washington Post*, November 30, 2019. https://www.washingtonpost.com/national/fifty-years-after-the-black-14-were-banished-wyoming-football-reckons-with-the-past/2019/11/30/fb7e9286-e93d-11e9-9c6d-436a0df4f31d_story.html.

Melas, Chloe. "NFL Commissioner Roger Goodell Says League Was Wrong for Not Listening to Players Earlier about Racism." *CNN*, June 6, 2020. https://www.cnn.com/2020/06/05/sport/roger-goodell-responds-nfl-stronger-together-video/index.html.

"Michael Jordan: 'I Can No Longer Stay Silent.'" *The Undefeated*, July 25, 2016. https://theundefeated.com/features/michael-jordan-i-can-no-longer-stay-silent/.

Moore, Louis. "Athletes Today Have a Lot to Learn from the 1968 NYAC Boycott." *The Shadow League*, February 16, 2018. https://theshadowleague.com/athletes-today-have-a-lot-to-learn-from-the-1968-nyac-boycott/.

Moye, David. "LeBron James Says Trump Doesn't 'Give a F**k about the People.'" *HuffPost*, February 15, 2018. https://www.huffpost.com/entry/lebron-james-donald-trump_n_5a8617cee4b05c2bcac92cf6.

NPR Staff. "Life after Iconic 1976 Photo: The American Flag's Role in Racial Protest." WBUR, September 18, 2016. https://www.wbur.org/npr/494442131/life-after-iconic-photo-todays-parallels-of-american-flags-role-in-racial-protes.

"Say Their Stories: Players and Coaches List." NFL.com, September 13, 2020. https://www.nfl.com/news/say-their-stories-players-and-coaches-list.

Schwab, Frank. "Hertz Made Advertising History with O. J. Simpson's Airport Runs." Yahoo! Finance, June 13, 2016. https://finance.yahoo.com/blogs/nfl-shutdown-corner/hertz-made-advertising-history-with-o-j--simpson-s-airport-runs-140015008.html.

Shapiro, Michael. "MLB Exec: Kneeling during National Anthem May Keep Teams from Signing Bruce Maxwell." *Sports Illustrated*, December 14, 2018. https://www.si.com/mlb/2018/12/14/bruce-maxwell-national-anthem-kneeling-free-agency-oakland-athletics-catcher-unsigned.

Smith, Gary. "The Chosen." Vault, *Sports Illustrated*, December 23, 1996. https://vault.si.com/vault/1996/12/23/the-chosen-tiger-woods-was-raised-to-believe-that-his-destiny-is-not-only-to-be-the-greatest-golfer-ever-but-also-to-change-the-world-will-the-pressures-of-celebrity-grind-him-down-first.

"Spain and Culture, in Aid of Basque Refugee Children (under the Auspices of the National Joint Committee for Spanish Relief)." Speech by Paul Robeson, Royal Albert Hall, June 24, 1937. https://memories.royalalberthall.com/content/spain-and-culture-aid-basque-refugee-children-under-auspices-national-joint-committee-0.

Steele, David. "After Another Police Shooting, Silence from Kaepernick's Critics Speaks Volumes." *Sporting News*, September 20, 2016. https://www.sportingnews.com/us/nfl/news/colin-kaepernick-critics-silence-tulsa-police-shooting-video-unarmed-trent-dilfer-drew-brees/3ctygu5rh54v1t5vi2wkl47gd.

———. "Colin Kaepernick, Bruce Maxwell Prove How Activism Can Shine without Stars." *Sporting News*, September 25, 2017. https://www.sportingnews.com/us/nfl/news/colin-kaepernick-nfl-national-anthem-protests-donald-trump-activism/n3iniij1ma9n1oxj4lniic7u1.

———. "Colin Kaepernick Mixed Up in Another Toxic 49ers Divorce." *Sporting News*, November 25, 2015. https://www.sportingnews.com/us/nfl

/news/49ers-colin-kaepernick-divorce-toxic-jed-york-jim-harbaugh
-smear-campaign/1l6ztdu45pwtd1ajw8tbjyw975.

———. "An Endless Fight, a Defining Choice." *Sporting News*, 2018. https://
www.sportingnews.com/us/nfl/features/sports-protest-anthem-history
-examples-kaepernick-lebron-trump-1968-olympics.

———. "Ex-NFL Anthem Protestor Applauds Colin Kaepernick and Athletes
Supporting Him." *Sporting News*, September 6, 2016. https://www.sport
ingnews.com/us/nfl/news/colin-kaepernick-national-anthem-protest
-david-meggyesy-support/arcnb0if71t51459swp2hwk0e.

———. "Jack Johnson Has Been Pardoned; Now It's Time to Immortalize
Him." *Sporting News*, May 26, 2018. https://www.sportingnews.com/us
/boxing/news/jack-johnson-donald-trump-pardon-statues-memorials
-rescue-legacy/1br4idr50quzs15fg8e0wqr62u.

———. "The Longer Colin Kaepernick Kneels, the More Truth He Drags Out
of Us." *Sporting News*, October 17, 2016. https://www.sportingnews.com
/us/nfl/news/colin-kaepernick-truth-national-anthem-protest-49ers
-bills/rrgsrpgy4nb81qnm0hg61es5v.

———. "Under Armour's Kevin Plank Should Have Listened to Stephen
Curry's Warning about Donald Trump." *Sporting News*, August 17, 2017.
https://www.sportingnews.com/us/nba/news/stephen-curry-kevin
-plank-under-armour-ceo-deal-president-donald-trump-quote-inter
view/ix39bmjnst941eqas6nll885v.

———. "With Boycotting Patriots Players, White House Visits No Longer
Routine." *Sporting News*, April 19, 2017. https://www.sportingnews.com
/au/nfl/news/patriots-white-house-visit-date-time-boycotting-players
-donald-trump-tom-brady/1k656704w4ner1g0xuolofdu3v.

Tackett, Michael. "Trump Welcomes the Red Sox to the White House, but
Not All of Them Are There." *New York Times*, May 9, 2019. https://www
.nytimes.com/2019/05/09/us/politics/boston-red-sox-white-house-visit
.html.

Wyche, Steve. "Colin Kaepernick Explains Why He Sat during National
Anthem." NFL.com, August 27, 2016. https://www.nfl.com/news/colin
kaepernick-explains-why-he-sat-during-national-anthem-0ap3000000
691077.

INDEX

David Steele has been a professional sports journalist for more than 35 years. He has written for the *Sporting News*, AOL, the *Baltimore Sun*, the *San Francisco Chronicle*, and *Newsday*, and has contributed to ESPN's *The Undefeated*, *USA Today*, and the NAACP's the *Crisis* magazine. He is the coauthor of *Silent Gesture: The Autobiography of Tommie Smith* (Temple) and of *Four Generations of Color*, the autobiography of pioneering baseball scout and sports agent Miles McAfee. He has won writing awards from the National Association of Black Journalists, the Association of Black Media Workers, the Associated Press Sports Editors, and the Society of Professional Journalists. A graduate of the University of Maryland at College Park, he serves on the advisory board for the Shirley Povich Center for Sports Journalism at his alma mater.